"I strongly recommend this book for every person who wants to be healthy while enjoying the sensation of sweetness as nature meant it to be enjoyed—with good, whole, safe food."

—A. Hoffer, M.D., Ph.D., author of *Orthomolecular Nutrition* and *Nutrients to Age without Senility*

"Karen Barkie has provided a delightful and helpful cookbook that will enable families to enjoy sweetened cakes, cookies, pies, custards, and desserts without sugar! Her book, *Sweet and Sugarfree*, furnishes simple recipes, easy to prepare, using common fruits. I highly recommend it."

—William G. Crook, M.D., author of *Tracking Down Hidden Food Allergy*

"By using fruits as sweetening agents, Karen E. Barkie succeeds in upgrading traditional dessert recipes. She is imaginative in utilizing the sweetness in fruits to create appealing dishes. She guides the reader along a path to create nutritious as well as delicious desserts—a commendable approach."

—Beatrice Trum Hunter, author of *The Great Nutrition Robbery*

"Karen Barkie combines common sense with her imaginative use of fruit as a sweetener to create delicious sugarfree desserts that are good for children."

—Jerome Vogel, M.D., medical director of The New York Institute for Child Development, Inc.

"Karen Barkie has done her homework most thoroughly. It is apparent that she is intimately acquainted with the complex problem of managing food allergy, food addiction, and allergy-like sensitivity to chemical additives. She displays great ingenuity in preparing a nicely diversified group of recipes for many excellent sugar and saccharin-free desserts."

"Karen Barkie's recipes are a satisfying alternative to traditional be-sugared desserts. I particularly commend them as the very healthiest for young children."

"League families will enjoy these recipes, which satisfy the sweet tooth in a nutritional way."

Sweet
and
Sugarfree

Sweet and Sugarfree

An All-Natural,
Fruit-Sweetened
Dessert Cookbook

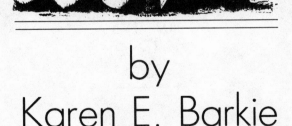

by
Karen E. Barkie

St. Martin's Press • New York

Library of Congress Cataloging in Publication Data

Barkie, Karen E.
Sweet and sugarfree.

Includes bibliographical references.
1. Desserts. 2. Cookery (Fruit) 3. Sugar-f
diet—Recipes. I. Title.
TX773.B36   641.8′6   82–5606
AACR2
ISBN 0-312-78065-6   10 9 8 7 6 5 4
ISBN 0-312-78066-4 (pbk.)   10 9

Design by Laura Hammond

To my children,
Scotty and Eric,
who inspired this work

Contents

INTRODUCTION

What mother does not want wholesome and nutritious foods for her family? Perhaps I went further than most in my prohibition of America's #1 high calorie nonfood: sugar. But my interest in nutrition led me to discover enough disturbing facts about sugar to make me firmly resolve to keep candy and Twinkies out of the mouths of my children.

You probably know that this substance—sugar—of which the average American consumes 128 pounds a year contains no vitamins or minerals. Perhaps you are also aware of the common health problems related to refined sugar, refining being the removal of all natural ingredients until the product is 99.9 percent pure sucrose— and empty calories. Sugar enters our bodies in an unnaturally concentrated form, putting a strain on the body. The initial "high" we receive from sugar is quickly followed by the "low" of fatigue, exhaustion, and irritability. We have less energy after eating sugar than before. It is not surprising that sugar consumption is related to health problems. Sugar has been linked to dental cavities, obesity, and diabetes. Its role in heart disease, hypoglycemia, allergies, hyperactivity, cancer, and other related health problems has been suggested and is being investigated.

To avoid the evils of sugar, many people turn to honey as an alternative sweetener. Unfortunately, honey offers only a small amount of vitamins and minerals in exchange for its 992 calories per cup. (A cup of sugar contains 751 calories.) The primary nutrients in honey are potassium, calcium, and phosphorus, but it would take more than 5 cups of honey to meet your recommended daily requirement of potassium, 12½ cups for calcium, and 16½ cups for phosphorus. Although it is believed to cause slightly less of a shock to the system than sugar, concentrated honey does stress the body. Like sugar, it can cause behavioral disturbances and mood fluctuations. Children are particularly susceptible, and many of us have seen our own children become active or disagreeable after a sugar or honey-filled snack. Along with cutting down sugar, The Feingold Association (which helps hyperactive children through dietary management) also recommends reducing consumption of honey and other simple sugars since they may trigger off hyperactive behavior.

So honey and sugar are, I learned, both unhealthful. Since I was no more willing to serve my family cancer-causing artificial sweeteners, I simply stopped serving cakes, cookies, candy, and other sugar-sweetened desserts, and my husband, two children, and I ate only fresh fruit for snacks and desserts. They seemed happy—for a while —and I was satisfied that we were eating nutritious foods.

But as the children grew, so too did their desire for more varied desserts. They were no longer satisfied with a banana or pear in their lunch box when the other children at school were eating cupcakes and popsicles. Even my husband was beginning to drop hints like "remember how good chocolate cake tastes?" And I had to admit I too missed desserts. It was time to reintroduce them, but I would not compromise my standards—they had to be nutritious. It was then that I turned to nature's most wholesome sweetener, available in a variety of colors and delicious flavors: fruit.

Whereas sugar supplies no vitamins and minerals and honey only small amounts, fruit is rich in them. Apricots, cantaloupe, peaches, mangoes, and papayas are rich in vitamin A—honey contains none. Fruits are our primary source of vitamin C. Fresh guavas, lemons, persimmons, papayas, strawberries, and oranges supply at least 50 times the vitamin C in honey (compared 100 gram weight each). Although honey does supply a small amount of iron, avocados, bananas, lemons, limes, strawberries, guavas, and persimmons all supply more. Peaches, strawberries, guavas, mangoes, avocados, bananas, blueberries, and sweet cherries are richer in essential B vitamins. Fruits also contribute healthful fiber along with their bounty of vitamins and minerals.

Moreover, fruit has considerably fewer calories than sugar or honey. Compared pound for pound, most fresh fruits contain less than 18 percent (and many much less) of the calories supplied by sugar. Few fruits contain more than 20 percent of the calories in an equal weight of honey, and many are surprisingly low. This comparatively low sugar content is even more significant since most fruit-sweetened desserts require only small amounts of fruit for full-bodied natural sweetness.

In contrast to the high calorie sweeteners, fruits possess the unique ability to sweeten without the unnaturally sugary sweet taste that has for too long characterized our desserts. The highly concentrated sweetness of sugar and honey masks the subtle and delicious flavors of whole grains, farm fresh eggs and milk, and nuts and seeds. Fresh fruit, however, is not unnaturally concentrated and possesses the ability to readily blend with other natural foods, to complement and contrast flavors, and to enhance the natural sweetness of desserts without drowning out the other wholesome ingredients. Without the intrusion of sugary sweetness, fruit-sweetened desserts come alive with the subtle blending of natural flavors. Each fruit contributes its own particular taste—some lightly sweet, others pleasantly tart or spicy—but each produces desserts that are as flavorful and varied as the many ingredients they contain.

High in vitamins and minerals and low in calories, fruit is an excellent sweetener, far more nutritious than sugar or honey. Encouraged by these findings and eager to serve wholesome desserts to my family, I began scouring bookstores and health-food stores for books using only fruit as a sweetener, and I was repeatedly discouraged. Some books called for honey, others for wine, but I could find no book that used fruit alone as a sweetener in desserts.

And so this book was born in my kitchen. From a few recipes it has grown to over 200, and from the first banana bread it has grown to include cakes, pies, cookies, sherbets, custards, and much more. During the two years I have spent developing the concept of fruit sweetening, my commitment to creating delicious, healthful, and visually appealing desserts steadily strengthened. Encouraged by the enthusiastic response of my friends and neighbors, I have expanded this work into a cookbook.

This collection of fruit-sweetened recipes offers a healthful alternative to traditional sugary, high-calorie desserts. People can now choose desserts without sacrificing good nutrition. Mothers can offer their families wholesome desserts, and at long last, children can be raised enjoying delicious desserts that are good for them. Even hyperactive children who are sensitive to food additives and follow the Feingold diet can enjoy fruit-sweetened desserts since all the ingredients are additive-free and many are composed of "allowable" fruits. Also, it is hoped that these recipes will offer the growing sugar-sensitive population (diabetics, hypoglycemics) desserts that are otherwise denied. (If you are under medical care, consult your physician before making any dietary changes.) This book is offered not only as a new option in dessert sweetening, but also as a contribution toward the improved nutrition and better health of us all.

Sweet
and
Sugarfree

Cakes and Coffee Cakes

Fruit-sweetened cakes are light and soft with delicious flavor. Hearty applesauce, light and delicate pear juice, and thick, sweet banana nectar are just a few of the fruit flavors that readily blend into unforgettable cake and coffee cake desserts.

Serve cakes, naturally sweetened with fruit, as a delicious and nutritious finish to dinner or lunch. Serve warm coffee cake, topped with spicy apple slices or packed full of plump blueberries, to your family for Sunday breakfast, to your weekly bridge club, to your neighbor when she drops by for coffee, or wrap one up to surprise your friends at the office. Wholesome and delicious fruit-sweetened cakes and coffee cakes are a welcome treat anytime—from your morning coffee break to your bedtime snack.

Helpful Hints

1. Always bake in a preheated oven.
2. Use recommended size baking pans.
3. Generously oil (or butter) and flour pans.

4. Spread batter evenly in the pans before baking.
5. When cake is done, it will pull slightly from the sides of the pan, turn lightly brown, and a knife inserted will come out clean.
6. Cakes prepared with blended fruit should be baked until well-browned unless otherwise noted.
7. Cool cake in the pan 5 minutes before turning out on a wire rack.
8. Cakes freeze well; wrap securely in aluminum foil.

Recipe Suggestions

Flour Substitutions—Refer to Fortify with Flour (see pages 140–142) for recommended flours, substitution guidelines, and suggested amounts.

Cake Mix-In—Any of the following may be stirred into cake batter for variety, taste, and nutritional value: raisins, carob chips, nuts, seeds, coconut, toasted oats, grated carrot, granola, chopped dates, chopped fresh fruit, nutmeg, or cinnamon.

Cake Bake-On—Smooth batter in baking pans. Generously sprinkle on spices, nuts, seeds, wheat germ, rolled oats, flaked coconut, chopped fresh fruit, or any Sprinkle-On Topping (see pages 127–128). Press topping gently into batter with the back of a spoon, and bake as directed.

Cake Toppings—Frost cakes with fruit pudding, softened cream cheese, jam, or choose a Spread-On or Spoon-On Topping (see pages 129–130).

APPLE ALMOND CAKE

Spicy and light apple flavor in a crunchy cake. Serve filled with creamy pudding.

Cake:
1½ cups unsweetened apple juice
1 cup rolled oats
¼ cup butter, softened
2 eggs
½ teaspoon vanilla extract
2½ cups unbleached white flour
¾ teaspoon baking soda
2 teaspoons baking powder
1 teaspoon cinnamon
1 teaspoon nutmeg
½ cup ground almonds

Topping:
1 recipe Apple Parfait Pudding, pages 93–94
1 fresh apple, peeled, cored, and sliced
⅓ cup slivered almonds

Beat together apple juice, rolled oats, butter, eggs, and vanilla extract. Add flour, baking soda, baking powder, spices, and ground almonds. Beat well. Spoon into two round 9" by 1½" cake pans that have been oiled and floured. Smooth batter in pans. Bake at 350 degrees for 20 to 25 minutes or until firm to the touch and a knife inserted in the center comes out clean. Cool on wire racks.

Prepare pudding as directed. To serve, spread chilled pudding between cake layers and over top. Garnish with sliced apple and almonds. Serves 8.

BANANA WALNUT CAKE

Rich banana flavor with light walnut crunch. Delicious with banana jam.

Cake:
⅔ cup mashed banana (mash ripe banana with a fork)
½ cup butter, softened
3 large eggs
¾ cup water
2 cups unbleached white flour
2 teaspoons baking powder
1 teaspoon baking soda
1 teaspoon cinnamon
1 cup chopped walnuts, or ½ cup walnuts and ½ cup raisins

In a mixing bowl beat together mashed banana and butter until creamy. Add eggs and water. Beat well. Stir in flour, baking powder, baking soda, and cinnamon. Beat until smooth. Add chopped walnuts. Spoon batter into an oiled and floured 9" by 13" baking pan. Spread batter evenly in pan. Bake at 350 degrees for 20 minutes or until a knife inserted comes out clean. Cool and cut into squares. Serves 8 to 10.

ORANGE BLUEBERRY CAKE

Sweet, colorful, and delicious with lots of fresh blueberries and coconut.

Cake:
3 large eggs
½ cup butter, softened
1 cup unsweetened orange juice
½ teaspoon orange extract
2½ cups unbleached white flour
1 teaspoon baking soda

2 teaspoons baking powder
1 teaspoon cinnamon
¼ teaspoon grated lemon rind
1 cup flaked coconut
1 cup fresh blueberries

Topping:
⅓ cup flaked coconut

Beat together eggs, butter, orange juice, and orange extract. Add flour, baking soda, baking powder, cinnamon, and grated lemon rind; beat well. Stir in 1 cup flaked coconut and blueberries. Spoon mixture into an oiled and floured 9" by 13" baking pan. Spread batter evenly in pan.

Sprinkle ⅓ cup flaked coconut over batter. Bake at 350 degrees for 20 to 25 minutes or until browned. Cool on a wire rack. Serves 8 to 10.

PINEAPPLE CARROT CAKE

Moist and spicy cake filled with shredded carrot.

Cake:
3 large eggs
½ cup butter, softened
1 cup unsweetened pineapple juice
2½ cups unbleached white flour
1 teaspoon baking soda
2 teaspoons baking powder

1 teaspoon nutmeg
1 teaspoon cinnamon
3 cups grated fresh carrot

Topping:
1 cup crushed pineapple, well drained
1 teaspoon cinnamon

Beat together eggs, butter, and pineapple juice. Add flour, baking soda, baking powder, and spices. Beat well. Stir in grated carrot and mix well. Spread batter evenly in an oiled and floured 9" by 13" baking pan. Toss topping ingredients together and sprinkle over batter. Bake at 350 degrees for 25 to 30 minutes or until browned. Cool on a wire rack. Serves 8 to 10.

VANILLA CAROB CAKE

A super-delicious, deep-brown cake with creamy frosting. Our traditional birthday cake.

Cake:
3 large eggs
⅓ cup mashed banana (mash ripe banana with a fork)
½ cup butter, softened
1¼ cups milk
2 teaspoons vanilla extract

2¼ cups unbleached white flour
¾ cup carob powder
2 teaspoons baking powder
1 teaspoon baking soda
1 cup flaked coconut

Frosting: Creamy Carob Frosting, page 129

To prepare cake beat together eggs, mashed banana, butter, and milk until creamy. Add vanilla extract, flour, carob powder, baking powder, and baking soda. Beat well. Stir in flaked coconut. Spoon batter evenly into an oiled and floured 9" by 13" baking pan. Bake at 350 degrees for 20 to 25 minutes or until a knife inserted comes out clean. Cool.

Prepare frosting and spread in a thin layer over cooled cake and serve. Serves 8 to 10.

FRUIT-SWEETENED CHEESECAKE

Light cheese flavor with fruit—a welcome dessert anytime.

Pastry:
1 egg yolk
¼ cup milk
1 cup unbleached white flour
½ teaspoon baking powder
1 teaspoon nutmeg

2 cups blended fruit (see recommendations below)
2 teaspoons vanilla extract
2 cups cottage cheese
3 tablespoons unbleached white flour

Filling:
4 eggs
1 or 2 teaspoons lemon juice

Topping:
Half of any fruit pudding recipe (see index)

To prepare crust, beat together egg yolk and milk. Add flour, baking powder, and nutmeg. Blend well. Pat evenly into the bottom of an oiled 9" spring-form pan.

To prepare filling, whip all ingredients in a blender or food processor. Pour into pastry-lined pan. Bake at 350 degrees for one hour and 25 minutes or until edges are browned. Turn off oven and leave to cool with door slightly open.

Spread pudding over cheesecake and refrigerate until serving. Serves 8.

• Recommended Fruit
Whip any of the following chopped fruit in a blender until smooth: apple, pear, pineapple, peach.

LEMON CAKE WITH PINEAPPLE GLAZE

A tangy, light, and fluffy cake with a warm, sweet, spicy topping.

Cake:

¼ cup vegetable oil (or butter, softened)

¼ cup mashed banana (mash ripe banana with a fork)

2 large eggs

3 tablespoons lemon juice

⅔ cup plain yogurt

¼ cup milk

1 teaspoon vanilla extract

1¾ cups unbleached white flour

1 teaspoon baking soda

2 teaspoons baking powder

Topping: Pineapple Glaze

1 6-oz. can unsweetened frozen pineapple juice concentrate

1 teaspoon cornstarch

½ teaspoon cinnamon

To prepare cake, beat together oil or butter, mashed banana, and eggs until creamy. Add lemon juice, yogurt, milk, and vanilla extract. Beat well. Measure remaining ingredients, add, and beat until smooth. Spoon batter into an oiled and floured 9″ round baking pan. Smooth batter evenly in pan. Bake at 350 degrees for 25 minutes or until nicely browned. Cool on a wire rack.

To prepare topping, combine ingredients in a small saucepan and whip with a whisk over medium heat until mixture thickens slightly. Remove from heat.

To serve, spoon Pineapple Glaze over warm cake. Serves 6.

CRANBERRY ORANGE CAKE

Sweet orange flavor in a hearty oat cake. Serve with whipped cream.

Cake:

1½ cups unsweetened orange juice

1 cup rolled oats

¼ cup butter, softened

2 large eggs

½ teaspoon orange extract

2½ cups unbleached white flour

1 teaspoon baking soda

2 teaspoons baking powder

1 cup sliced fresh cranberries

Topping: Creamy Orange Topping, page 130

Beat together orange juice, rolled oats, butter, eggs, and orange extract. Add flour, baking soda, baking powder, and sliced cranberries. Beat well. Spoon into oiled and floured 9" by 13" baking pan. Spread batter evenly in pan. Bake at 350 degrees for 25 to 30 minutes or until browned. Cool on a wire rack.

To serve, cut cake into bars and top with a spoonful of topping. Serve immediately. Serves 8 to 10.

GEORGIA PEACH CAKE

Thin and light cake layers topped with sweet peaches and whipped cream.

Cake:
2 large eggs
¾ cup blended peach (whip chopped fresh or canned peach in a food processor or blender until smooth)
⅓ cup butter, softened
1 cup water
2⅓ cups unbleached white flour

1 teaspoon baking soda
2 teaspoons baking powder
2 teaspoons cinnamon

Filling:
1 29-oz. can sliced peaches in unsweetened juice (or 3½ cups)
½ pint heavy cream
1 teaspoon vanilla extract

In a mixing bowl beat together eggs, blended peach, and butter until creamy. Add water, flour, baking soda, baking powder, and cinnamon. Beat well. Spoon batter evenly into two oiled and floured 9" round cake pans. Bake at 350 degrees for 15 to 20 minutes or until very lightly browned and a knife inserted comes out clean. Cool on wire racks.

To serve, drain canned peaches. If slices are thick, cut them in half lengthwise. Place a cake layer on a serving plate, spread half of the sliced peaches evenly on top, and repeat with remaining cake layer and peaches. Whip cream and vanilla extract until mixture is fluffy and peaks form. Drop by spoonfuls over cake. Serves 8.

CREAMY PINEAPPLE CAKE

Soft, thin layers of delicious pineapple cake filled and topped with sweet pudding.

Cake:

2 large eggs

¾ cup blended pineapple (whip unsweetened canned pineapple and juice in a food processor or blender until smooth)

¼ cup vegetable oil

1 cup milk

¼ teaspoon orange extract

2⅓ cups unbleached white flour

1 teaspoon baking soda

2 teaspoons baking powder

½ teaspoon cinnamon

½ cup flaked coconut

Topping: 1 recipe Pineapple Pudding, page 96

Beat together eggs, blended pineapple, oil, milk, and orange extract. Add flour, baking soda, baking powder, and cinnamon. Beat well. Stir in flaked coconut. Spoon into two oiled and floured round 9" by 1½" baking pans. Spread batter evenly in pans. Bake at 350 degrees for 15 minutes or until browned and a knife inserted comes out clean. Cool on wire racks.

To serve, spread pudding between and over cake layers. Garnish with fresh fruit or flaked coconut as desired. Serves 8.

STRAWBERRY BANANA CAKE

Two soft banana cake layers filled and topped with fresh strawberries and whipped cream.

Cake:

1 cup mashed banana (mash ripe banana with a fork)

¼ cup vegetable oil

2 large eggs

⅓ cup plain yogurt

1½ cups unbleached white flour

1 teaspoon baking soda

2 teaspoons baking powder

Filling:

1 pint fresh strawberries (wash, remove stems, and slice thin)

Topping:

½ pint heavy cream, whipped until fluffy

To prepare cake, beat together mashed banana, oil, eggs, and yogurt until creamy. Add flour, baking soda, baking powder, and beat well. Spoon into two round, oiled and floured 9" cake pans. With a spatula smooth the batter evenly in pans. Bake at 350 degrees for 15 minutes or until a knife inserted comes out clean. Cool.

To serve, slice the strawberries into a bowl. Crush a few with the back of a spoon to make a sauce and generously spoon over bottom cake layer. Top with remaining cake layer, the rest of the strawberries and the whipped cream. Serve immediately. Serves 8.

APPLE PRUNE COFFEE CAKE

Spicy and rich. Delicious warm.

Cake:
½ cup butter, softened
3 large eggs
¼ teaspoon orange extract
1 cup unsweetened apple juice
2½ cups unbleached white flour
1 teaspoon baking soda

2 teaspoons baking powder
1 teaspoon nutmeg
1 teaspoon cinnamon
1 cup diced prunes
½ cup chopped walnuts

Topping: Apple Spice Topping, page 127

In a medium-sized mixing bowl beat together butter, eggs, orange extract, and apple juice. Add flour, baking soda, baking powder, and spices; beat well. Stir in diced prunes and nuts. Spoon into an oiled and floured 9" by 13" baking pan. Spread batter evenly in pan.

Prepare topping as directed and sprinkle over batter. Bake at 350 degrees for 20 minutes or until a knife inserted comes out clean. Cool on wire rack and cut into bars. Serves 8 to 10.

APPLE RAISIN COFFEE CAKE

Sweet and chewy cake with spicy apple flavor.

Cake:
3 large eggs
⅔ cup unsweetened apple juice
¼ cup butter, softened
2 cups unbleached white flour
½ teaspoon baking soda
1 teaspoon baking powder
½ teaspoon nutmeg
1 teaspoon cinnamon
¾ cup raisins

Topping:
1 cup apple, peeled, cored, and
    thinly sliced
1 teaspoon lemon juice
Cinnamon

In a mixing bowl combine eggs, apple juice, and butter and beat well. Add flour, baking soda, baking powder, and spices. Mix thoroughly and stir in raisins. Spoon into an oiled and floured round 9" by 1½" baking pan and spread batter evenly in pan. (Batter will fill the pan upon baking so use less batter if substituting a shallower or smaller pan.)

Toss topping ingredients together in a small bowl. Arrange apple slices over batter in an attractive pattern. Sprinkle with additional cinnamon. Bake at 350 degrees for 20 minutes or until browned and a knife inserted comes out clean. Cool on wire rack. Serves 6.

DATE COFFEE CAKE

A sweet coffee cake filled with chopped dates.

Cake:
⅓ cup mashed banana (mash ripe
    banana with a fork)
½ cup butter, softened
3 large eggs
1 teaspoon vanilla extract
1¼ cups water
3 cups unbleached white flour
1 teaspoon baking soda
2 teaspoons baking powder
1½ cups chopped dates

Topping:
⅓ cup chopped dates
⅓ cup chopped walnuts
⅓ cup flaked coconut

Beat together mashed banana and butter until creamy. Add eggs, vanilla extract, and water; beat. Measure in flour, baking soda, and baking powder, and beat well. Stir in 1½ cups chopped dates. Spoon batter into an oiled and floured 9" by 13" baking pan. Spread batter evenly in pan.

Combine topping ingredients and sprinkle over batter. Bake at 350 degrees for 20 to 25 minutes or until a knife inserted comes out clean. Cool on wire rack. Serves 8 to 10.

HAWAIIAN COFFEE CAKE

A delightful coffee cake filled with coconut and fruit.

Cake:
2 large eggs
⅔ cup unsweetened pineapple juice
¼ cup butter, softened
2 cups unbleached white flour
½ teaspoon baking soda
2 teaspoons baking powder

1 cup crushed pineapple, well drained
1 cup flaked coconut

Topping:
½ teaspoon cinnamon
½ cup crushed pineapple, well drained

In a mixing bowl beat together eggs, pineapple juice, and butter. Add flour, baking soda, and baking powder; beat well. Stir in 1 cup crushed pineapple and flaked coconut. Spoon into an oiled and floured 9" round pan. Spread batter evenly.

Toss topping ingredients together and sprinkle over batter. Bake at 350 degrees for 20 to 25 minutes or until firm to the touch. Cool on wire rack. Serves 6.

Cookies

Warm cookies, fresh from the oven and sweetened with fruit, are as delicious a dessert as a child could wish for. The nutritional value of fruit-sweetened cookies makes them a wholesome addition to a meal and a good quality snack by themselves. Nuts, oats, fruit, and flaked coconut all contribute toward delicious, healthful, and flavorful cookies. Pack fruit-sweetened cookies into lunch boxes, fill up the cookie jar for afternoon snacks, and share some with toddlers, knowing you are supplying your kids with a nutritious treat. Bring homemade cookies to the art meeting, mix up a batch for the picnic, and freeze extra for company next week. Let the kids help in preparing these delicious cookies that will please the whole family from the "nutritious"-conscious mother to the "delicious"-conscious kids!

Helpful Hints

1. Unless otherwise specified, oil baking sheets before baking.
2. Always bake in a preheated oven.
3. It is advisable to check cookies as they bake since some burn easily.
4. Remove cookies to a wire rack to cool after baking.

5. Allow cookies to cool completely before storing.
6. Freeze extra cookies in sealed containers.

Recipe Suggestions

Flour Substitutions—Refer to Fortify with Flour (see pages 140–142) for recommended flours, substitution guidelines, and suggested amounts.

Cookie Mix-In—To boost the nutritional value of cookies as well as to add inviting flavors and textures, stir any of the following into the batter and bake: carob chips, rolled oats, chopped fresh fruit, granola, flaked coconut, chopped nuts, spices, chopped dates, raisins, or grated carrot.

Cookie Bake-On—Drop cookie batter onto baking sheets as directed. For variety and texture sprinkle cookies with any of the following: rolled oats, seeds, spices, wheat germ, raisins, chopped nuts, flaked coconut, chopped dates, chopped fresh fruit, or any Sprinkle-On Topping (see pages 127–128). Press topping gently into cookie batter with the back of a spoon and bake as directed.

Cookie Toppings—Any of the following are ideal cookie frostings. Simply spread over cookies individually or spread over half and cover with remaining cookies for filled cookie sandwiches: jam, nut butter, cream cheese, fruit pudding, or choose any Spread-On Topping (see page 129).

APPLESAUCE GRANOLA COOKIES

Moist and chewy cookies filled with applesauce and granola. Kids love them!

2 large eggs

2 tablespoons vegetable oil

1 cup unsweetened applesauce

2 tablespoons unsweetened frozen concentrated apple juice

2 cups unbleached white flour

½ teaspoon baking powder

1 teaspoon cinnamon

½ teaspoon nutmeg

2 cups unsweetened granola (see Note, page 15)

In a mixing bowl beat together eggs, oil, applesauce, and apple juice concentrate. Add flour, baking powder, and spices. Beat well. Mix in granola. Drop batter by teaspoons onto oiled baking sheets. Bake at 350 degrees for 7 to 10 minutes or until firm to the touch and bottoms are browned. Cool on wire racks. Yields 4 dozen.

• Note

To prepare homemade, unsweetened granola, combine equal amounts of any of the following: rolled oats, chopped nuts, flaked coconut, finely chopped dried fruit, seeds.

BROWNIE CAROB OATMEALS

Delicious cookies that bake up light with rich brownie flavor.

½ cup mashed banana (mash ripe banana with a fork)
⅓ cup vegetable oil
¼ teaspoon vanilla extract
2 large eggs
¼ cup milk
1¼ cups unbleached white flour
¼ cup carob powder
¼ teaspoon baking soda
1 cup chopped nuts
⅔ cup rolled oats

In a medium-sized mixing bowl beat together mashed banana, oil, vanilla extract, eggs, and milk until creamy. Add flour, carob powder, and baking soda. Beat well. Stir in chopped nuts and rolled oats. Mix well. Drop batter by small teaspoonfuls onto oiled baking sheets. Bake at 350 degrees for 8 to 10 minutes or until just firm to the touch. Cool on wire racks. Yields 4 dozen.

CAROB CHIP COOKIES

Sweet cookies with carob chips.

¼ cup mashed banana (mash ripe banana with a fork)
¼ cup vegetable oil
1 large egg
1 cup unbleached white flour
1 cup rolled oats
¾ cup carob chips

Beat together mashed banana and oil until creamy. Beat in egg. Add flour, rolled oats, and carob chips. Mix well. Drop batter by teaspoons onto oiled baking sheets. Bake at 350 degrees for 10 minutes or until cookies just start to brown around the edges. Cool on wire racks. Yields 36 cookies.

CASHEW CRUNCHIES

Fresh roasted flavor in a nourishing treat.

Cookies:
4 eggs
1 tablespoon unsweetened fruit juice
2/3 cup unbleached white flour

1/4 teaspoon baking soda
2 cups ground cashew nuts

Topping:
Cashew halves

Beat together eggs and fruit juice. Add flour, baking soda, and ground nuts. Beat well. Drop batter by teaspoons onto oiled baking sheets. Top each cookie with a cashew half. Bake at 375 degrees for 5 to 8 minutes or until just firm, but not browned. Cool on wire racks. Yields 4 dozen.

HARVEST COOKIES

Light spicy flavor in a nutritious squash- and date-filled cookie.

Cookies:
1/3 cup vegetable oil
1 large egg
1 cup squash, cooked, drained, and mashed
1 1/2 cups unbleached white flour

1/2 teaspoon baking powder
1 teaspoon nutmeg
1/2 teaspoon cinnamon
1 1/2 cups finely chopped dates

Topping:
Walnut pieces

Beat together oil, egg, and squash. Add flour, baking powder, and spices. Beat well and stir in chopped dates. Drop batter by small teaspoonfuls onto oiled baking sheets. Top each cookie with a walnut piece. Bake at 350 degrees for 10 minutes or until firm to the touch. Cool on wire racks. Yields 3 dozen.

LEMON MOONS

Large, cakelike cookies with the tang of lemon and the sweetness of pineapple juice.

Cookies:
4 large eggs
½ cup vegetable oil
1 6-oz. can unsweetened frozen concentrated pineapple juice

⅓ cup lemon juice
2 cups unbleached white flour
½ teaspoon baking powder

Topping:
Grated lemon rind

In a mixing bowl beat together eggs, oil, pineapple concentrate, and lemon juice. Add flour and baking powder. Beat well. Drop batter by teaspoonsfuls onto oiled baking sheets and sprinkle grated lemon rind over each cookie. Bake at 375 degrees for 8 minutes or until cookies are slightly raised and firm to the touch. (Do not overcook as bottoms will burn.) Carefully remove from baking pans and place on wire racks to cool. Yields 5 dozen cookies.

• Variations

Orange Sours—Prepare as directed above, using unsweetened frozen concentrated orange juice. Top with grated orange rind.

Tangy Apple Cookies—Prepare as directed above using unsweetened frozen concentrated apple juice. Sprinkle each cookie with cinnamon before baking.

PINEAPPLE COOKIES

Light pineapple flavor in a soft, tasty cookie.

Cookies:
¼ cup mashed banana (mash ripe banana with a fork)
¼ cup unsweetened frozen concentrated pineapple juice
¼ cup vegetable oil
1 large egg

1 tablespoon milk
1 cup unbleached white flour
¼ teaspoon baking soda
½ cup flaked coconut

Topping:
Grated orange rind

In a medium-sized mixing bowl beat together mashed banana, pineapple juice concentrate, oil, egg, and milk until creamy. Add flour, baking soda, and flaked coconut. Beat well. Drop by rounded teaspoonfuls onto oiled baking sheets and sprinkle with grated orange rind. Bake at 350 degrees for 8 minutes or until just brown around the edges and firm to the touch. Cool on wire racks. Yields 25 to 30 cookies.

PEANUT BUTTER COOKIES

Rich peanut flavor in a light, soft cookie.

¼ cup mashed banana (mash ripe banana with a fork)	2 tablespoons butter, softened
½ cup peanut butter	1 cup unbleached white flour
2 large eggs	½ teaspoon baking powder
¾ teaspoon vanilla extract	½ teaspoon nutmeg
	1 cup chopped peanuts

In a mixing bowl beat together mashed banana, peanut butter, eggs, vanilla extract, and butter until creamy. Add flour, baking powder, and nutmeg. Beat well. Stir in chopped peanuts. Drop batter by rounded teaspoonfuls onto lightly oiled cookie sheets. Press each cookie down with the back of a fork and again in the opposite direction to indent a checkered pattern into each cookie. (Wet the fork with cold water occasionally to avoid sticking.) Bake at 375 degrees for 5 to 8 minutes or until lightly browned. Cool on wire racks. Yields 2 to 3 dozen.

SUNFLOWER CRUNCHIES

An intriguing, crunchy texture.

1 cup unbleached white flour	¼ cup chopped nuts
1 cup sunflower seeds (chop in a food processor or blender)	⅓ cup blended fruit (whip chopped fruit in a food processor or blender until smooth)
¼ cup vegetable oil	

In a mixing bowl combine flour, chopped sunflower seeds, oil, and nuts. Gradually add blended fruit, using just enough to form a loose dough. Pinch together bits of the batter and shape into 1″ balls. Place on oiled baking sheets and flatten down each cookie with the back of a fork. (Dip the fork in cold water occasionally to avoid sticking.) Bake at 350 degrees for 10 minutes or until firm to the touch. Cool on wire racks. Yields about 30 cookies.

Custards and Gelatin Desserts

Custards

Fruit-sweetened custards are nutritious, light, satin-smooth, and delicious. Whether apple, pear, peach, or pineapple, fruit adds a distinctive zing and flavor to plain custards.

Serve custards sprinkled with nutmeg or piled high with whipped cream and smothered with fresh fruit for wholesome and adaptable desserts. Custards are rich with milk goodness, perfect for a light lunch with fruit and cheese or as a finale to dinner. Top with yogurt, canned fruit, or granola for a satisfying snack at any time of day.

Helpful Hints

1. In preparing custards, use fresh fruit sauces and fresh eggs and milk for the finest quality.
2. To vary recipes, add cinnamon, nutmeg, cloves, or ginger; stir in flaked coconut; add a combination of fruit sauces rather than a single sauce; sprinkle with finely ground wheat germ or nuts.

3. When the custard has set, the top is lightly browned and creased around the edges. A knife inserted in the center comes out clean.
4. Custards may be served often to contribute valuable protein, vitamins, and minerals to the family's diet.
5. Do not freeze custards. They lose texture, flavor, and appeal if frozen.
6. Always refrigerate custard desserts.

Some Fruits Suitable for Custards

apple	mango	peach	pineapple
banana	papaya	pear	

Recipe Suggestion

Sauced Custard—To perk up a custard with a splash of classic fruit flavor, simply slice through the custard with a knife in vertical slits. Pour your choice of fruit sauce over the custard. Thin sauces such as strawberry or blueberry are generally preferable not only for their ability to flow well but also for their enticing colors. Chill thoroughly. Shortly before serving top with whipped cream and a few fresh berries. Sprinkle with grated nutmeg and serve.

SPICY APPLESAUCE CUSTARD

A light, sweet custard dessert.

1½ cups unsweetened applesauce   *4 eggs*
1 cup milk   *1 teaspoon cinnamon*

Whip the above ingredients together in a blender until smooth. Pour into six 8-oz. glass custard cups, sprinkle with cinnamon, and place on a large baking pan with 1″ of hot water in it. Bake at 350 degrees for 45 minutes or until custard has set. Cool and refrigerate.

To serve, top each custard with a spoonful of applesauce and chopped nuts. Serves 6.

BANANA COCONUT CUSTARD

My family's favorite custard. Tastes too delicious to be so good for you!

3 eggs
2 ripe bananas, cut in pieces
1½ cups milk
1 teaspoon nutmeg
½ teaspoon baking powder
⅓ cup unbleached white flour
1 cup flaked coconut

Blend eggs and banana pieces until smooth in a blender. Add remaining ingredients and blend. Pour into six 8-oz. custard cups, sprinkle with additional nutmeg and place in a large baking pan with 1″ of hot water in it. Bake at 350 degrees for 45 minutes or until custard has set. Cool and refrigerate. Serves 6.

PINEAPPLE SAUCE CUSTARD

Sweet and tangy pineapple makes a wonderful custard.

1½ cups blended pineapple (whip a can of crushed pineapple and juice in a blender until smooth)
1½ cups milk
3 eggs
1 teaspoon vanilla extract

Whip the above ingredients together in a blender, pour into six 8-oz. custard cups, sprinkle with nutmeg, and place in a large pan with 1″ of hot water in it. Bake at 350 degrees for 45 minutes or until custard has set. Cool and refrigerate.

To serve, top each chilled custard with flaked coconut. Serves 6.

RICH PEAR CUSTARD

Distinctive pear flavor in a creamy dessert.

1½ cups blended pear (whip chopped fresh or canned pear in a blender or processor)
1 cup milk
4 eggs
½ teaspoon nutmeg
¼ teaspoon cinnamon

Whip the above ingredients together in a blender and pour into six 8-oz. custard cups. Sprinkle with additional nutmeg. Place in large baking pan filled with 1" of hot water. Bake at 350 degrees for 45 minutes or until custard has set. Cool and refrigerate.

To serve, top each custard with Nutty Pear Topping (see page 128). Serves 6.

Gelatin Desserts

Fruit juices and gelatin combine with whipped cream, meringue, nuts, and fresh fruit to create attractive and elegant desserts. Prepare in an attractive mold and surprise your guests with a dessert that is both healthful and delicious. Serve with cottage cheese or a wedge of cheddar as a nutritious, light meal. As a welcome follow-up to a filling meal, a colorful addition to a buffet table, or a complement to a summer lunch, gelatin molds are delightful any time of the year. Substitute and mix fruit juices, beat in meringues and creams, stir in flaked coconut, sliced fruit, and chopped nuts to create your own appealing desserts.

Helpful Hints

1. Sprinkle gelatin over cold water and allow to soften several minutes before combining with boiling water.
2. Pineapple juice must be boiled 2 or 3 minutes to destroy an enzyme that interferes with proper gelation.
3. To chill gelatin mixture quickly, place bowl in ice water and stir often.
4. For fancy fruit patterns, fill mold with a thin layer of gelatin mixture. When it is partially gelled, arrange fruit slices in the mold and gently pour in remaining gelatin mixture. Chill until firm.
5. To layer gelatin desserts, allow first layer to chill until almost firm. Pour over it the second layer that has been chilled slightly. Refrigerate until firm.
6. Before adding chopped fruit or nuts, allow gelatin mixture to chill

until it reaches the consistency of unbeaten egg white. Gently stir in filling and refrigerate.

7. To remove gelatin from mold, place mold in warm water for a few seconds, cover with the serving dish, and invert together. Remove mold and serve.

APPLE WALNUT DESSERTS

Nuts and bits of apple in a light, apple-flavored gelatin.

Gelatin:
¼ cup unsweetened apple juice, chilled

1 package (1 tablespoon) unflavored gelatin

1¾ cups unsweetened apple juice

Filling:
½ cup chopped walnuts
½ cup chopped fresh apple

Topping:
½ pint heavy cream

Pour chilled apple juice in a small bowl and sprinkle over it the unflavored gelatin. Mix and allow to set 2 or 3 minutes to soften. Meanwhile, heat apple juice to a boil. Mix together gelatin mixture and boiling apple juice, cool, and refrigerate.

When mixture reaches the consistency of unbeaten egg whites, remove from the refrigerator and stir in chopped walnuts and apple. Evenly divide among six 8-oz. custard cups and return to refrigerator. Chill.

To serve, whip heavy cream until fluffy and spoon over individual custards. Sprinkle with cinnamon if desired. Serves 6.

CRANBERRY APPLE MOLD

Light apple sweetness in a cranberry nut dessert.

Gelatin:
¼ cup unsweetened apple juice, chilled

1 package (one tablespoon) unflavored gelatin

1¾ cups unsweetened apple juice

Filling:
½ pint heavy cream
1 cup sliced fresh cranberries

Topping:
⅓ cup ground nuts

Sprinkle gelatin over chilled apple juice, mix well, and allow to stand 2 or 3 minutes until softened. Bring apple juice to a boil, combine with gelatin mixture and mix well. Pour into a bowl and refrigerate.

When mixture reaches the consistency of unbeaten egg white, remove from the refrigerator. Whip cream until light and fluffy, combine with gelatin mixture, and beat at low speed just until blended. Return to refrigerator to chill just a short while. Stir in sliced cranberries and return to refrigerator in a dessert mold to chill until firm.

To serve, unmold the gelatin onto a dessert plate and sprinkle with ground nuts. Serves 6.

ELEGANT ORANGE PARFAIT

A favorite company dessert. Sherbet-like orange flavor in a creamy white gelatin. Serve in champagne glasses and top with fruit.

Gelatin:

¼ cup unsweetened orange juice, chilled

1 package (1 tablespoon) unflavored gelatin

1¾ cups unsweetened orange juice

Filling:

½ pint heavy cream

Topping:

1 small can orange segments in unsweetened juice

Pour ¼ cup chilled orange juice in a bowl and sprinkle gelatin over it. Mix well and allow gelatin to soften 2 or 3 minutes. Meanwhile bring 1¾ cups of orange juice to a boil. Gradually add to gelatin mixture, stirring well. Cool and refrigerate until mixture reaches a consistency slightly thicker than unbeaten egg white.

Beat heavy cream in a small bowl until light and fluffy. Combine with gelatin mixture and beat on low speed just until blended thoroughly. Spoon mixture into champagne glasses or dessert goblets, refrigerate, and chill until firm.

To serve, top each portion with a well-drained, chilled orange segment. Sprinkle with cinnamon if desired. Serves 6.

PINEAPPLE CRÈME

A very light dessert with a blend of vanilla, cream, and pineapple flavors. Delicious!

Gelatin:
¼ cup cold water
1 package (1 tablespoon) unflavored gelatin
1¼ cups pineapple juice

Filling:
8 ounces (1 cup) sour cream
2 teaspoons vanilla extract

Topping:
1 ripe banana, sliced
¼ cup slivered almonds

In a small bowl sprinkle gelatin over cold water and mix well. Allow to set 2 or 3 minutes to soften. Bring pineapple juice to a boil and boil 2 minutes. (Pineapple juice must boil 2 minutes to destroy an enzyme that interferes with proper gelation.) Combine boiling pineapple juice and gelatin mixture. Stir well and refrigerate.

When mixture reaches the consistency of unbeaten egg white, whip together sour cream and vanilla until fluffy. Add gelatin mixture and mix just until thoroughly blended. Return bowl to refrigerator and chill until firm.

To serve, spoon cream out into dessert goblets, top with sliced banana, and sprinkle with slivered almonds. Serves 4 to 6.

• Variations

After combining gelatin mixture and sour cream mixture return bowl to the refrigerator and allow to chill a short while. Remove and stir in any of the following: one cup sliced banana, chopped nuts, flaked coconut. Return to the refrigerator and chill until firm.

SOUR ORANGE DESSERT

Tangy orange and sour cream flavors.

Gelatin:
¼ cup unsweetened orange juice, chilled
1 package (1 tablespoon) unflavored gelatin
1¼ cups unsweetened orange juice

Filling:
8 ounces (1 cup) sour cream
2 teaspoons vanilla extract
¼ teaspoon grated orange peel

Topping:
Orange segments, fresh or canned, unsweetened

In a small bowl sprinkle gelatin over chilled orange juice and mix well. Allow to set 2 or 3 minutes to soften. Bring orange juice to a boil, combine with gelatin mixture, and mix well. Refrigerate.

When mixture reaches the consistency of unbeaten egg white, remove from refrigerator. Beat together sour cream, vanilla extract, and grated orange rind. Add gelatin mixture and beat just until mixed. Pour mixture into a dessert mold, return to the refrigerator, and allow to chill until firm.

To serve, unmold dessert on a serving plate and garnish plate around mold with orange segments. Serves 4.

APPLE SPICE MOLD

Zesty lemon and apple meet in a very light dessert.

Gelatin:
¼ cup chilled lemon juice
1 package (1 tablespoon) unflavored gelatin
1¼ cups unsweetened apple juice

2 egg whites (from large eggs)

Filling:
1½ cups chopped apple
¼ teaspoon cinnamon

Pour lemon juice in a small bowl and sprinkle gelatin over it. Mix well and allow to stand 2 or 3 minutes to soften. Bring apple juice to a boil, combine with gelatin mixture, and mix well. Cool and refrigerate.

When gelatin mixture reaches the consistency of unbeaten egg white, remove from the refrigerator. Whip egg whites until peaks form, add gelatin mixture, and beat on low speed just until well blended. Return to chill a *short* while.

Toss chopped apple with cinnamon and stir into gelatin mixture. Spoon into dessert mold and chill. Invert onto a serving plate. Serves 6.

PINEAPPLE CREAM DESSERT

For special occasions.

Gelatin:
¼ cup cold water
1 package (one tablespoon) unflavored gelatin
1¾ cups unsweetened pineapple juice

Filling:
½ pint heavy cream

Topping:
½ pint heavy cream
½ teaspoon orange extract
Grated lemon rind

Sprinkle gelatin over cold water, mix, and allow to stand 2 or 3 minutes to soften. Bring pineapple juice to a boil and boil 2 minutes. (Pineapple juice must be boiled 2 minutes to destroy an enzyme that interferes with gelation.) Combine boiling juice with gelatin mixture and mix well. Cool and chill.

When mixture reaches the consistency of unbeaten egg white, remove from the refrigerator. Beat heavy cream at high speed in a small bowl until fluffy. Combine with gelatin mixture and beat on low speed just until blended. Pour into dessert goblets and refrigerate until firm.

To serve, whip heavy cream and orange extract until light and fluffy. Top each dessert with a generous serving of whipped cream topping and sprinkle lightly with grated lemon rind. Serves 6.

Dessert Bars

If you want a savory, wholesome dessert without any fuss, then dessert bars are for you. Packed full of fruit, nuts, seeds, flaked coconut, spices, or grains, this baked dessert is a fiber-filled, nutritious delight. A favorite with kids, dessert bars make a great after-school snack, and pack easily into lunch boxes and picnic baskets. Serve this tasty, family-style treat plain or frosted with nut butter, jam, cream cheese, or fruit spread.

Helpful Hints

1. Always bake in a preheated oven.
2. Bake in size pan specified.
3. Generously grease and flour pans.
4. With a spatula spread batter evenly in the pan before baking.
5. Unless otherwise noted, allow dessert bars to cool before cutting.
6. Allow to cool thoroughly before storing.
7. Wrap tightly in aluminum foil to freeze.

Recipe Suggestions

Flour Substitutions—Refer to Fortify with Flour (see pages 140–142) for recommended flours, substitution guidelines, and suggested amounts.

Dessert Bar Mix-In—The following may be stirred into batter for variety and added nutritional value: granola, flaked coconut, jam, nuts, raisins, whole berries, spices, herbs, chopped dates, chopped fresh fruit, peanut butter, or roasted soybeans.

Dessert Bar Bake-On—For a baked-on topping, smooth batter evenly in the baking pan and sprinkle on spices, nuts, seeds, wheat germ, rolled oats, flaked coconut, chopped fresh fruit, bits of jam, carob chips, or a Sprinkle-On Topping (see pages 127–128). Press topping gently into batter with the back of a spoon and bake as directed.

Dessert Bar Toppings—Frost cooled dessert bars with the following or use as a filling between two bars: jam, nut butter, cream cheese, fruit pudding, cottage cheese, or one of the Spread-On Toppings (see page 129).

APPLE RAISIN BARS

Moist and spicy bars filled with raisins.

Cake:
½ cup unsweetened applesauce
½ cup unsweetened apple juice
3 eggs
¼ cup butter, softened
2 cups unbleached white flour
1 teaspoon baking soda

2 teaspoons baking powder
1 teaspoon nutmeg
1½ teaspoons cinnamon
1 cup raisins

Topping:
Cinnamon

In a mixing bowl beat together applesauce, apple juice, eggs, and butter until well blended. Add flour, baking soda, baking powder, and spices. Beat thoroughly. Stir in raisins. Spoon batter into an oiled and floured 8″ square baking pan and sprinkle with additional cinnamon. Bake at 350 degrees for 25 minutes or until a knife inserted comes out clean. Cool. Serves 6.

PINEAPPLE BLUEBERRY BARS

A bar packed with blueberries and pineapple.

Bars:

1/4 cup blended pineapple (whip canned unsweetened crushed pineapple and juice in food processor or blender until smooth)

1 large egg

1/2 cup unsweetened pineapple juice

1/4 teaspoon orange extract

1 tablespoon vegetable oil

1 1/2 cups unbleached white flour

1 teaspoon baking soda

1 teaspoon baking powder

1/2 cup whole fresh blueberries (wash, and discard any damaged ones)

1/3 cup well-drained crushed pineapple

Beat together blended pineapple, egg, pineapple juice, orange extract, and oil. Add flour, baking soda, and baking powder and beat well. Stir in blueberries and crushed pineapple. Spoon batter into an oiled and floured 8″ square baking pan. Smooth batter in the pan. Bake at 350 degrees for 20 to 25 minutes or until browned and a knife inserted comes out clean. Cool on a wire rack. Serves 6.

BANANA COCONUT BARS

Moist, but light.

Bars:

1/3 cup vegetable oil

1 cup mashed banana (mash ripe banana with a fork)

2 large eggs

1/2 cup milk

1/4 teaspoon lemon juice

1 3/4 cups unbleached white flour

1 teaspoon baking soda

2 teaspoons baking powder

1 cup flaked coconut

Topping:

1/2 cup flaked coconut

Beat together vegetable oil and mashed banana until creamy. Add eggs, milk, and lemon juice; beat well. Measure in flour, baking soda, and baking powder and beat. Stir in 1 cup flaked coconut. Spoon batter into an oiled and floured 9″ by 13″ baking pan. Spread batter evenly in pan and sprinkle with 1/2 cup flaked coconut. Bake at 350 degrees for 15 to 20 minutes or until browned. Cool and cut into bars. Serves 8 to 10.

CASHEW BARS

Crunchy cashews in a delicious bar.

Bars:

½ cup butter, softened

½ cup mashed banana (mash ripe banana with a fork)

¾ cup water

3 large eggs

2 cups unbleached white flour

1 teaspoon baking soda

2 teaspoons baking powder

1 teaspoon nutmeg

1 cup ground cashews

Topping:

½ cup ground cashews

Beat together butter and mashed banana. Add water and eggs. Beat well. Measure in flour, baking soda, baking powder, nutmeg, and 1 cup ground cashews and beat. Spoon batter into an oiled and floured 9″ by 13″ baking pan. Sprinkle with ½ cup ground nuts. Bake at 350 degrees for 20 minutes or until lightly browned. Cool on wire racks and cut into bars. Serves 8 to 10.

COCONUT PINEAPPLE SQUARES

Sweet, chewy squares filled with coconut and pineapple bits.

Squares:

3 large eggs

½ cup butter, softened

1 cup pineapple juice (drained from 20-oz. can of unsweetened crushed pineapple)

2½ cups unbleached white flour

1 teaspoon baking soda

2 teaspoons baking powder

1 teaspoon cinnamon

2 cups flaked coconut

Well-drained crushed pineapple (from 20-oz. can)

Topping:

½ cup flaked coconut

Beat together eggs, butter, and pineapple juice. Add flour, baking soda, baking powder, and cinnamon. Beat well and stir in 2 cups coconut and crushed pineapple. Spoon batter into an oiled and floured 9″ by 13″ baking pan. Spread batter evenly in pan and sprinkle with ½ cup coconut. Bake at 350 degrees for 20 to 25 minutes or until browned. Cool and cut into squares. Serves 8 to 10.

DATE GRANOLA SQUARES

Delicious squares packed full of crunchy granola and sweet dates.

Squares:
2 large eggs
¼ cup butter, softened
1½ cups unsweetened pear juice
2½ cups unbleached white flour
1 cup unsweetened granola (see Note below)
1 teaspoon baking soda
2 teaspoons baking powder
1 cup chopped dates
1 teaspoon cinnamon
¼ teaspoon ginger
1 teaspoon nutmeg

Topping:
½ cup chopped dates
½ cup unsweetened granola

In a medium-sized mixing bowl beat together eggs, butter, and pear juice. Add flour, granola, baking soda, baking powder, 1 cup dates, and spices. Beat thoroughly. Spoon batter into an oiled and floured 9″ by 13″ baking pan and spread batter evenly with a spoon. Sprinkle topping ingredients over the batter and bake at 350 degrees for 20 minutes or until a knife inserted into the batter comes out clean. Cool and cut into squares. Serves 8 to 10.

• Note
To make your own unsweetened granola, combine equal amounts of any of the following: rolled oats, chopped nuts, flaked coconut, sesame seeds, chopped sunflower seeds, dried fruit.

ORANGE CRANBERRY NUT BARS

Sweet and spicy orange bars with the tang of cranberries.

Cake:
3 large eggs
⅔ cup orange juice
¼ cup butter, softened
¼ teaspoon orange extract
2 cups unbleached white flour
1 teaspoon cinnamon
½ teaspoon baking soda
1 teaspoon baking powder
1 cup diced fresh cranberries

Topping:
¼ teaspoon nutmeg
⅓ cup finely chopped walnuts

In a mixing bowl beat together eggs, orange juice, butter, and orange extract. Add flour, cinnamon, baking soda, and baking powder. Beat well. Mix in cranberries. Spoon into an oiled and floured 8″ square baking pan. Spread batter evenly in pan.

Combine topping ingredients and sprinkle evenly over batter. Bake at 350 degrees for 20 minutes or until a knife inserted in the center comes out clean. Cool on wire rack. Serves 6.

CHEWY PEAR BARS

Large "sandwich" bars filled with date spread.

Bars:

1 cup blended pear (whip chopped fresh or canned pear in a food processor or blender until smooth)

2 large eggs

⅓ cup vegetable oil

1½ cups unbleached white flour

1 cup rolled oats

2 teaspoons baking powder

Nutmeg

Filling:

Date Spread (see page 106)

Beat together blended pear, eggs, and oil until creamy. Add flour, rolled oats, and baking powder. Beat until well mixed. Oil and flour two 8″ square baking pans. Spoon half of the batter into each pan and smooth evenly. Sprinkle with nutmeg. Bake at 350 degrees for 20 minutes or until nicely browned and firm to the touch. Cool on wire racks.

Cut each cake square into six bars (cut in half in one direction and in thirds in the other). Spread date filling on half the bars and cover with remaining bars. Serves 6.

PEANUT BUTTER BANANA SQUARES

A delicious combination of flavors.

Squares:

1 large egg

¼ cup peanut butter

1 cup mashed banana (mash ripe banana with a fork)

¼ cup milk

1 cup unbleached white flour

1 teaspoon baking soda

1 teaspoon baking powder

½ cup chopped peanuts

Topping:

Sweet Banana Jam (see page 105)

Beat together egg, peanut butter, and mashed banana until creamy. Add milk and beat. Measure in flour, baking soda, and baking powder. Beat well. Stir in chopped nuts. Spoon into an oiled and floured 8" square baking pan. Spread batter evenly in pan. Bake at 350 degrees for 20 minutes or until browned. Cool.

Cut into squares and top each with a dab of jam. Serves 6.

PINEAPPLE PIE SQUARES

Fancy pastry squares filled with sweet pineapple.

Squares:

3 egg yolks

¾ cup milk

¼ teaspoon almond extract

2 teaspoons baking powder

3 cups unbleached white flour
(approximately)

Filling:

one 20-oz. can unsweetened crushed
pineapple

1½ tablespoons cornstarch

To prepare pastry, beat together egg yolks, milk, and almond extract. Add baking powder and gradually add flour, adding just enough to form a soft dough. Mix well. Divide in half and roll each half out on a floured surface to approximately 9" by 13". Place bottom piece in an oiled and floured 9" by 13" baking pan, pressing dough ½" up the sides.

To prepare filling, drain can of crushed pineapple and catch juice in a bowl. Combine juice and cornstarch in a small saucepan and heat over medium setting. Stir as mixture thickens. Remove thickened liquid from heat and add crushed pineapple. Mix well and spoon evenly into pastry-lined baking pan. Cover with top pastry and crimp edges together where top and bottom pastry meet to seal in filling. Bake at 350 degrees for 25 minutes or until lightly browned. Cool and cut into squares. Serves 8 to 10.

• Variations

Sprinkle over pineapple filling chopped nuts, spices, dried fruit, or coconut and cover with top crust.

SESAME BARS

Sesame seeds top a soft banana bar.

Bars:
2 large eggs
¼ cup mashed banana (mash ripe banana with a fork)
¼ cup butter, softened
¼ cup water

1 cup unbleached white flour
½ teaspoon baking soda
½ teaspoon baking powder
½ teaspoon nutmeg

Topping:
¼ cup sesame seeds

In a mixing bowl beat together eggs and mashed banana until creamy. Add butter and water and beat. Measure in flour, baking soda, baking powder, and nutmeg. Beat well. Oil an 8″ square baking pan. Sprinkle half of the sesame seed topping evenly over the bottom of the oiled pan. Add the batter and gently spread over seeds until smooth. Sprinkle with remaining seeds. Bake at 350 degrees for 15 minutes. Cool and cut into bars. Serves 6.

TROPICAL FRUIT BARS

A delicious blend of pineapple, nuts, and coconut.

Bars:
2 large eggs
1 tablespoon vegetable oil
1 tablespoon unsweetened frozen pineapple juice concentrate
1 teaspoon lemon juice
1¼ cups unbleached white flour

1 teaspoon baking soda
1 cup flaked coconut
¾ cup chopped nuts
one 15-oz. can unsweetened crushed pineapple

Topping:
¾ cup chopped nuts

Beat together eggs, oil, pineapple juice concentrate, and lemon juice. Add flour, baking soda, flaked coconut, ¾ cup chopped nuts, and crushed pineapple (including juice). Mix well. Spoon mixture evenly into an oiled and floured 9″ by 13″ baking pan. Sprinkle with ¾ cup chopped nuts. Bake at 350 degrees for 15 to 20 minutes or until firm. Cool and cut into bars. Serves 8 to 10.

ZINGY CITRUS BARS

Moist, crunchy, and fruity. Makes a big batch.

Bars:

2 large eggs
¼ cup butter, softened
1½ cups unsweetened orange juice
½ teaspoon orange extract
2½ cups unbleached white flour
1 teaspoon baking soda
2 teaspoons baking powder
½ teaspoon cinnamon
½ teaspoon nutmeg
1 cup chopped fresh cranberries
1 cup chopped walnuts

Topping:

¾ cup flaked coconut
¾ cup crushed pineapple, well drained

Beat together eggs, butter, orange juice, and orange extract. Add flour, baking soda, and baking powder. Measure in spices and beat well. Stir in chopped cranberries and chopped nuts. Spoon mixture into an oiled and floured 9" by 13" baking pan. Spread batter evenly in pan.

Sprinkle flaked coconut and drained pineapple over batter. Bake at 350 degrees for 20 to 25 minutes or until a knife inserted comes out clean. Cool and cut into bars. Serves 8 to 10.

Muffins

Fresh warm muffins are an old-fashioned favorite; sweetened and flavored with fruit, nuts, and seeds, they are a nourishing, hearty treat. Especially delicious fresh from the oven, fruit-sweetened muffins will make any breakfast special, and are a wholesome snack and inviting addition to any meal. They also freeze well, so make an extra batch for a handy lunch box treat.

Helpful Hints

1. Grease muffin wells thoroughly and coat with flour.
2. Always bake in a preheated oven.
3. When muffins are done they are browned and firm to the touch, and a knife inserted in the center of one comes out clean.
4. Allow muffins to rest in the pan several minutes before removing.
5. To remove muffins from the pan, loosen the edges with a sharp knife, invert the pan, and tap the bottom gently.
6. Serve warm, or cool and frost. Cool completely before storing and store refrigerated.

Recipe Suggestions

Flour Substitutions—Refer to Fortify with Flour (see pages 140–142) for recommended flours, substitution guidelines, and suggested amounts.

Muffin Mix-In—Stir any of the following into batter for variety and appeal: nuts, seeds, wheat germ, flaked coconut, carob chips, chopped dates, granola, whole berries, sliced fresh fruit, raisins, grated lemon or lime rind, or spices.

Muffin Bake-On—Before baking, sprinkle any of the following over muffins: nuts, wheat germ, rolled oats, flaked coconut, seeds, chopped dates, chopped fresh fruit, raisins, spices, or one of the Sprinkle-On Toppings (see pages 127–128). Press topping gently into muffin batter with the back of a spoon and bake as directed.

Muffin Toppings—After baking, frost with any of the following: nut butter, cream cheese, jam, fruit pudding, or a Spread-On Topping (see page 129).

Muffin'n Jam—Any homemade muffin can be perked up with a bright, sweet jam center. Simply pour half of the required batter into a muffin tin, carefully place a spoonful of jam in the center of each muffin, and cover with remaining batter. Bake as directed. For added sweetness, frost slightly warm muffins with jam and serve plain or sprinkled with flaked coconut, ground nuts or seeds, nutmeg, or cinnamon.

Muffin'n Nut Butter—Prepare as directed in previous recipe using nut butter in place of jam. Try peanut butter, cashew butter, or almond butter.

Pudding Muffins—With a small, sharp knife, cut a circle into the top of a cooled muffin, cutting down ¾ of the way into the muffin. Gently cut out this central cylinder, leaving a hole through the center, but not to the bottom. Fill to the top with cooled fruit pudding. Cut off the top crust of the removed muffin cylinder and place on top of the pudding. Serve immediately or chill. Jams and nut butters also make suitable fillings.

APPLESAUCE MUFFINS

Very soft and spicy with applesauce and raisins.

Muffins:
1 large egg
2 tablespoons vegetable oil
1½ cups unsweetened applesauce
2 cups unbleached white flour
¾ teaspoon baking soda
2 teaspoons baking powder
½ teaspoon nutmeg
½ teaspoon cinnamon
¾ cup raisins

Topping:
1 8-oz. package cream cheese, softened
Milk

Beat together egg, oil, and applesauce. Add flour, baking soda, baking powder, and spices; beat well. Stir in raisins. Spoon batter into oiled and floured muffin wells. Bake at 375 degrees for 20 to 25 minutes or until firm to the touch and browned. Cool on wire racks.

To make topping, cream together cream cheese and just enough milk to make a thick, spreadable mixture. Spread over cooled muffins and serve. Serves 12.

BLUEBERRY BANANA MUFFINS

Large, light, and sweet muffins.

Muffins:
⅔ cup mashed banana (mash ripe banana with a fork)
1 large egg
½ cup milk
⅓ cup vegetable oil
2 cups unbleached white flour
1 teaspoon baking soda
1 teaspoon baking powder
1 cup whole fresh blueberries (wash, and discard any damaged fruit)

Beat together mashed banana and egg until creamy. Add milk and oil; beat well. Measure in flour, baking soda, and baking powder. Beat well. Gently mix in blueberries. Spoon batter into oiled and floured muffin tins. Bake at 350 degrees for 15 minutes or until lightly browned. Cool on wire racks.

Serve plain or frost with jam or fruit butter. Serves 12.

LIGHT CAROB MUFFINS

Sweet carob and banana flavors combine in these light muffins.

Muffins:
½ cup mashed banana (mash ripe banana with a fork)
3 tablespoons vegetable oil
1 large egg
1 cup milk
¼ teaspoon vanilla extract
1½ cups unbleached white flour
¼ cup carob powder
1 teaspoon baking soda
2 teaspoons baking powder
½ cup flaked coconut

Topping:
½ pint heavy cream
½ teaspoon vanilla extract
3 tablespoons carob powder

Beat together mashed banana, oil, and egg until creamy. Add milk and vanilla extract and beat. Measure in flour, ¼ cup carob powder, baking soda, and baking powder. Beat well, and stir in flaked coconut. Pour batter into oiled and floured muffin tins. Bake at 350 degrees for 15 minutes or until firm to the touch. Cool on wire racks.

To prepare topping, beat ingredients together at high speed in a small bowl just until fluffy. Spread over muffins and serve. Serves 12.

ORANGE CRANBERRY MUFFINS

Large, golden, orange-flavored muffins with crisp cranberry tartness.

Muffins:
3 large eggs
½ cup butter, softened
1 cup unsweetened orange juice
2½ cups unbleached white flour
1 teaspoon baking soda
2 teaspoons baking powder
1 cup chopped fresh cranberries

Topping: Cranberry Cheese Nut Spread, page 129

Beat together eggs, butter, and orange juice. Add flour, baking soda, and baking powder; beat well. Stir in 1 cup chopped cranberries. Spoon into oiled and floured muffin wells. Bake at 350 degrees for 20 minutes or until muffins are firm to the touch and lightly browned. Cool on wire racks.

Prepare topping as directed and frost over cooled muffins. Sprinkle each with ground nuts. Serves 14.

SESAME MUFFINS

Mild sesame flavor and crunch.

Muffins:
3 eggs
¼ cup butter, softened
⅔ cup unsweetened fruit juice (apple, orange, pineapple, pear, etc.)

2 cups unbleached white flour
1 teaspoon baking powder
½ teaspoon baking soda
½ cup sesame seeds

Topping:
¼ cup sesame seeds

Beat together eggs, butter, and fruit juice. Add flour, baking powder, and baking soda. Beat well. Stir in ½ cup sesame seeds. Spoon batter into oiled and floured muffin tins and sprinkle batter with sesame seed topping. Bake at 350 degrees for 10 minutes or until lightly browned. Cool on wire racks. Serves 12.

PEACH AND CRANBERRY MUFFINS

Large, moist, and soft.

Muffins:
1 large egg
2 tablespoons vegetable oil
1½ cups blended peach (whip chopped fresh or canned peach in a food processor or blender)
2 cups unbleached white flour
1 teaspoon baking soda

2 teaspoons baking powder
1 teaspoon cinnamon
½ cup flaked coconut
1 cup diced fresh cranberries

Topping:
1 recipe Peach Butter (see page 107)
⅓ cup flaked coconut

Beat together egg, oil, and blended peach. Add flour, baking soda, baking powder, and cinnamon. Beat well. Stir in ½ cup flaked coconut and cranberries. Spoon batter into oiled and floured muffin tins. Bake at 350 degrees for 15 minutes or until browned. Cool.

To serve, frost muffins with Peach Butter and sprinkle with ⅓ cup flaked coconut. Serves 12.

PEAR PUDDING MUFFINS

Kids love these big pudding-filled treats.

Muffins:

3 large eggs

1 cup unsweetened pear juice

½ cup butter, softened

2½ cups unbleached white flour

2 teaspoons baking powder

1 teaspoon baking soda

1 teaspoon nutmeg

Filling:

1 recipe Fresh Pear Pudding (see pages 94–95)

Beat together in a medium-sized mixing bowl eggs, pear juice, and butter. Add flour, baking powder, baking soda, and nutmeg. Beat well. Spoon into oiled and floured muffins tins, filling wells half full. Bake at 350 degrees for 20 minutes or until lightly browned. Cool on wire racks.

Prepare pudding as directed, and chill. With a small, sharp knife cut out the center of each muffin in a circular shape, cutting down ¾ of the way into muffin and leaving the bottom intact. Carefully remove cylinder of muffin and generously fill with chilled fruit pudding. Slice the browned top crust off removed cylinder and place over pudding. Serves 10 to 12.

SAUCY PEAR MUFFINS

Light pear flavor with dates.

Muffins:

1 large egg

2 tablespoons vegetable oil

1½ cups blended pear (whip chopped fresh or canned pear in a food processor or blender)

2 cups unbleached white flour

1 teaspoon baking soda

2 teaspoons baking powder

½ teaspoon nutmeg

1 cup chopped dates

Topping:

Nutmeg

In a medium-sized mixing bowl beat together egg, oil, and blended pear. Add flour, baking soda, baking powder, and ½ teaspoon nutmeg. Beat well. Stir in dates. Spoon into oiled and floured muffin wells and sprinkle with nutmeg. Bake at 350 degrees for 15 minutes or until lightly browned. Cool on wire racks. Serves 12.

PEANUT BUTTER SURPRISE MUFFINS

Banana and peanut butter muffins with sweet jam centers.

Muffins:
1/4 cup mashed banana (mash ripe banana with a fork)
1/4 cup peanut butter
2 large eggs
1/3 cup vegetable oil
1 cup milk

2 cups unbleached white flour
1 teaspoon baking powder
1 teaspoon baking soda
1 cup chopped peanuts

Filling:
Jam, Fruit Butter, or Spread (see page 102)

Beat together in a medium-sized bowl mashed banana, peanut butter, and eggs until well blended and creamy. Add oil and milk and beat. Measure in flour, baking powder, and baking soda. Beat. Stir in chopped peanuts. Oil and flour muffin tins. Fill each well 1/3 full of batter. Spoon 1/2 teaspoon of jam or other filling into the center of each muffin and top with additional batter, filling wells 2/3 full. Bake at 350 degrees for 15 minutes or until browned. Cool.

To serve, frost with jam. Serves 12.

PINEAPPLE MUFFINS

Spicy muffins filled with bits of moist, sweet fruit.

Muffins:
1/2 cup butter, softened
3 large eggs
1 cup unsweetened pineapple juice (drained from 20-oz. can of crushed pineapple)
1 teaspoon lemon juice
2 1/2 cups unbleached white flour

1 teaspoon baking soda
2 teaspoons baking powder
1 cup well-drained crushed pineapple (from 20-oz. can)

Topping:
8-oz. package cream cheese, softened
1/2 cup ground pecans

Beat together butter, eggs, pineapple juice, and lemon juice. Add flour, baking soda, and baking powder. Beat well. Stir in crushed pineapple. Spoon batter into oiled and floured muffin tins. Bake at 350 degrees for 20 minutes or until lightly browned. Cool on wire racks.

Frost with cream cheese and sprinkle liberally with ground nuts. Serves 14.

Dessert-Style Pancakes

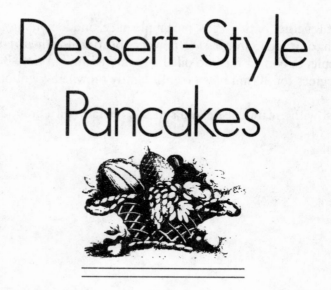

Hot off the griddle and steaming with warm fruit fragrance, pancakes are not only delicious, but can be as simple or as fancy a dessert as you desire. Spread with jam or homemade syrup, or, for an elegant finale to a meal, layer with whipped cream, drown in fruit sauce, and garnish with a scoop of sherbet.

And don't forget breakfast! This versatile dessert is also a highly nutritious way to begin the day. Enriched with nuts, seeds, fresh fruit, yogurt, or fruit juice, fruit-sweetened pancakes are a welcome change for breakfast. Also serve pancakes as a change for lunch and as a satisfying evening snack with friends, letting them garnish their own from a variety of toppings.

Helpful Hints

1. Grease a flat, heavy-bottomed frying pan. Cast iron is excellent.
2. Preheat pan over medium heat before adding batter.
3. If batter is thick, simply spread it out in the frying pan with the back of a spoon to form a large, flat pancake.

4. Cook on one side until bubbles appear through the flapjack and the bottom edges are browned. Turn over with a spatula.

5. Remove with a spatula to serving dishes and serve immediately —plain or with your favorite topping.

Recipe Suggestions

Flour Substitutions—Refer to Fortify with Flour (see pages 140–142) for recommended flours, substitution guidelines, and suggested amounts.

Pancake Mix-In—The following may be stirred into pancake batter for variety: wheat germ, flaked coconut, granola, raisins, rolled oats, whole berries, spices, carob chips, nuts, seeds, grated carrot, chopped dates, or chopped fruit.

Pancake Bake-On—Spoon batter onto hot griddle and cook on one side. Before turning over, sprinkle pancake with seeds, nuts, rolled oats, flaked coconut, spices, chopped dried fruit, bits of jam, chopped fresh fruit, or a Sprinkle-On Topping (see pages 127–128). Press topping down into pancake with the back of the spatula, flip, and cook until done. Serve topping side up.

Pancake Toppings—Top pancakes with any of the following: fruit sauces, fruit puddings, custards, jams, chopped fruit, cottage cheese, cinnamon, ice cream, sherbet, nuts, seeds, flaked coconut, nut butters, yogurt, toasted oat flakes, wheat germ, grated carrot, raisins, or a Spread-On or Spoon-On Topping (see pages 129–130).

Lone Flapjack—Place a single hot pancake on a dessert plate, top with your choice of topping, pie filling, sherbet, or spread.

Pancake Stack—Place a hot pancake on a serving dish, spread generously with your choice of filling, and repeat using two or three pancakes. Top with fruit sauce, whipped cream, or meringue. Serve immediately.

Flapjack Roll—Place a large, thin pancake on a dessert plate. Spoon one or two tablespoons of pudding, jam, or nut butter in the center. Gently roll to form a cylinder with filling inside. Place seam side down on serving dish. Spoon warm fruit sauce over filled pancake and serve immediately, garnished with fruit or nuts if desired.

HOMEMADE PANCAKE SYRUPS

Apricot Syrup (tart)—Combine one cup chopped dried apricots and one cup water in a small saucepan, bring to a boil, and simmer 20 minutes, covered. Cool; whip contents in a blender. Add about 1½ cups water or enough to reach syrup consistency. Store refrigerated. Yields 3 cups.

Currant Syrup (sweet)—Combine one cup currants with one cup water in a small saucepan, bring to a boil, and simmer 20 minutes, covered. Cool; whip in a blender. Store refrigerated. Yields 1 cup.

Date Syrup (sweet)—Combine one cup pitted dates and one cup water in a small saucepan, bring to a boil, and simmer 20 minutes, covered. Cool and whip contents in a blender. Add about ¾ cup water or enough to reach syrup consistency. Store refrigerated. Yields 2 cups.

Fig Syrup (sweet)—Combine one cup figs and one cup water in a small saucepan, bring to a boil, and simmer 20 minutes, covered. Cool and whip contents in a blender. Add one cup water or enough water to reach syrup consistency. Store refrigerated. Yields 2½ cups.

Pineapple Syrup (sweet)—Combine one cup dried pineapple and one cup water in a small saucepan, bring to a boil, and simmer 20 minutes, covered. Cool and whip contents in a blender. Add about one cup water or enough to reach syrup consistency. Store refrigerated. Yields 2½ cups.

Raisin Syrup (sweet)—Combine one cup raisins and one cup water in a small saucepan, bring to a boil, and simmer 20 minutes. Cool and whip contents in a blender. Add about ¼ cup water or enough to reach syrup consistency. Store refrigerated. Yields 1⅓ cups.

• To Make Sweeter Syrup

Substitute unsweetened fruit juice for water in the above recipes. For even sweeter syrup, unsweetened frozen fruit juice concentrate may be substituted for a portion of the liquid.

• To Serve

Heat syrup in a covered saucepan over low heat, stirring occasionally, until warm. Spoon generously over pancakes.

BANANA NUT PANCAKES

Banana slices and nuts in a delicious pancake.

2 eggs	1 tablespoon baking powder
1½ cups milk	3 bananas, sliced
2 tablespoons vegetable oil	1 cup chopped nuts
2 cups unbleached white flour	

In a mixing bowl beat together eggs, milk, and oil. Add flour and baking powder and mix well. Stir in sliced bananas and nuts. Pour by ¼ cupfuls onto hot, oiled griddle and cook until browned. Spoon warm Date Syrup over pancakes. Yields 14 pancakes.

CHEESE PANCAKES

Smooth and light with a taste of fruit. A fine dessert pancake.

⅔ cup cottage cheese	2 tablespoons vegetable oil
¼ cup unsweetened frozen fruit juice concentrate	1 cup unbleached white flour
2 eggs	1 teaspoon baking powder
	Nutmeg

In a blender whip together cottage cheese, fruit juice concentrate, eggs, and oil. Pour mixture into a bowl, combine with flour and baking powder, and beat. Drop by tablespoonfuls onto hot, oiled

griddle (medium setting). Sprinkle each pancake with nutmeg. After flipping and cooking completely, serve nutmeg side up. Yields 18 pancakes.
• Recommended Fruit Juice Concentrates
Apple, grapefruit, orange, pineapple.

FRUIT NUT PANCAKES

Chopped nuts and fruit in large sweet pancakes. Kids love these for breakfast.

1 cup milk	*1 tablespoon baking powder*
1 egg, beaten	*1 cup chopped nuts or raisins*
3 tablespoons vegetable oil	*1 cup chopped fruit, well drained*
2 cups unbleached white flour	

Beat together milk, egg, and oil. Add flour and baking powder and mix well. Stir in chopped nuts and fruit. Drop by ¼ cupfuls onto hot, oiled griddle. Batter will be thick so you may wish to spread out pancakes with the back of a spoon. Cook until browned. Spoon warm Raisin Syrup over pancakes. Yields 11 large pancakes.
• Recommended Chopped Fruit
Apple, whole berries, banana, peach, pear, pineapple.

FRUIT SAUCE PANCAKES

Choose any suggested fruit for these.

3 tablespoons vegetable oil	*2 eggs*
2 cups blended fruit (whip chopped fresh or canned fruit in a blender until smooth)	*1½ cups unbleached white flour* *1¾ teaspoons baking powder*

Beat together oil, blended fruit, and eggs. Add flour and baking powder; mix just until blended. Cook batter on hot, oiled griddle, using ¼ cup batter for each. Spoon warm Pineapple Syrup over pancakes. Yields 10 pancakes.
• Recommended Fruit
Banana, peach, apple, pear, pineapple.

HARVEST PANCAKES

Hearty, spicy, pumpkin pie flavor.

2 cups squash (cooked, drained and   *2 cups unbleached white flour*
   mashed)   *1 tablespoon baking powder*
3 eggs   *2 teaspoons nutmeg*
½ cup vegetable oil

In a large mixing bowl beat together squash, eggs, and oil. Add flour, baking powder, and nutmeg and mix well. Spoon by ¼ cupfuls onto an oiled, hot griddle. Flatten each pancake with the back of a spoon. They will rise well. Turn and cook until browned. Spoon warm Raisin Syrup over pancakes. Yields 12 pancakes.

FRUITY YOGURT PANCAKES

Thick, filling pancakes with mild yogurt and fresh fruit flavor.

2 eggs   *¼ teaspoon baking soda*
2 tablespoons vegetable oil   *¼ cup unsweetened fruit juice*
1 cup plain yogurt   *Nutmeg*
2 cups unbleached white flour

In a mixing bowl beat together eggs and oil. Add yogurt, flour, baking soda, and fruit juice and beat just until blended. Drop batter by ¼ cupfuls onto hot, oiled griddle. Sprinkle pancakes lightly with nutmeg. Turn, continue cooking, and serve nutmeg side up. Spoon warm Apricot Syrup over pancakes. Yields 9 pancakes.

• Recommended Fruit Juice

Apple, pear, orange, grapefruit, pineapple, papaya.

Pastries, Crêpes, and Turnovers

Homemade pastries sweetened with fruit and fruit juices are melt-in-your-mouth delicious and are easier to prepare than you'd think. What could be better than a fancy fruit turnover for brunch or a homemade éclair to top off a special meal? And who would have dreamed that pastry could be good for you? These are!

Helpful Hints

1. Always bake in a preheated oven.
2. When puff pastries are done, slice a slit in each with a knife, return to the turned-off oven, and leave 15 minutes with door ajar to dry and crisp.
3. Before filling, gently scoop out any pastry that is moist and discard it.
4. Fill just before serving for a moist, rich filling and crisp, light pastry. If filled and allowed to sit, pastry will become soggy.
5. To freeze, seal pastry shells in airtight containers or wrap in aluminum foil.

6. For crisper pastry shells, place in 325 degree oven for 5 minutes before filling and serving.

Recipe Suggestions

Flour Substitutions—Refer to Fortify with Flour (see pages 140–142) for recommended flours, substitution guidelines, and suggested amounts.

Pastry Fillings—The following filling suggestions should be added shortly before serving. Try mixing fillings or layering them. Recommended fillings include custard, jam, nut butter, yogurt, ice cream, sherbet, fruit pudding, chopped dried fruit, sliced fresh fruit, or any one of the Spread-On or Spoon-On Toppings (see pages 129–130).

Pastry Toppings—Place filled pastry on a serving dish. Spoon over any of the following: yogurt, fruit sauce, fruit pudding, or your favorite Spoon-On Topping (see pages 129–130). Sprinkle with carob chips, spices, sliced fresh fruit, chopped dried fruit, grated carrot, wheat germ, granola, flaked coconut, chopped nuts, seeds, or a Sprinkle-On Topping (see pages 127–128), and serve immediately.

PUFF PASTRY (OIL)

Light, rich pastry. From basic recipe make cream puffs and éclairs.

¼ cup unsweetened fruit juice　　*1 cup unbleached white flour*
¾ cup water　　*4 eggs*
½ cup vegetable oil

Bring fruit juice, water, and oil to a boil in a medium-sized saucepan. Add flour and with a fork mix until thoroughly blended and a soft, loose dough forms. Remove from heat and cool five minutes. Add eggs, one at a time, beating with a fork after each addition, until mixture is thoroughly blended. Bake pastry dough as suggested in the following recipes. Yields one recipe puff pastry.

PUFF PASTRY (BUTTER)

A light pastry with subtle butter flavor.

½ cup butter   1 cup unbleached white flour
1 cup boiling water   4 eggs

In a medium-sized saucepan combine butter and boiling water. Heat to a boil. Turn heat to low, add flour, and stir until mixture is thoroughly blended and a ball of dough forms. Remove from heat and allow to cool slightly. Add eggs, one at a time, and beat thoroughly after each addition with a fork until mixture forms a cohesive dough. Bake pastry dough as directed in the following recipes. Yields one recipe puff pastry.

• For Preparing a Day Ahead

Make pastry one day, refrigerate overnight, reheat at 325 degrees for 5 minutes, cool, and form and bake as directed.

PUFF PASTRY CREAM PUFFS

Firm cream puffs with sweet fruit filling. A holiday favorite.

1 recipe Puff Pastry   1 recipe Fruit Pudding (see pages 91–96)

Drop puff pastry dough by rounded tablespoonfuls onto oiled baking sheets about 3″ apart. Shape each cream puff with a knife into a mound that points up in the center. Bake in hot oven at 400 degrees for 5 minutes (or until tops start to brown), then reduce heat to 350 degrees and bake 25 minutes longer or until nicely browned and firm to the touch. For crispy pastry remove from the oven and with a sharp knife make a slit in the side of each one. Return to the turned-off oven with the door slightly open and leave 15 minutes to dry and crisp.

To prepare for serving, cut the top off each cream puff and remove any moist pastry inside. Fill each puff generously with fruit pudding and cover with pastry top. Place on dessert dishes and top with any whipped cream topping, ice cream, sherbet, or blended fruit. Serve the puffs soon after filling them. Pastry will become soggy if allowed to set. Yields 25 cream puffs.

MINI–CREAM PUFFS

Small, delicate puffs for bite-size desserts.

Prepare as directed above; however, drop by rounded teaspoons (not tablespoons) onto oiled baking sheets and bake at 400 degrees for 5 minutes, reduce heat to 350 degrees, and continue baking until golden brown.

To serve, fill as directed above and serve at buffets, parties, and holiday gatherings. Yields 50 puffs.

PUFF PASTRY ÉCLAIRS

Who can resist éclairs?

1 recipe Puff Pastry   *1 recipe Fruit Pudding (see pages 91–96)*

Prepare puff pastry as directed. On an oiled baking sheet, drop two tablespoons of batter next to each other. With a knife blend the two together to form into an oblong mound that points up to the center along the center ridge. Repeat, filling the baking sheet with oblong pastry mounds. Bake at 400 degrees for 5 minutes, lower heat to 350 degrees, and continue baking for 25 minutes or until golden brown. For crispy pastry, remove from the oven and with a sharp knife make a slit in the side of each one. Return to the turned-off oven with the door slightly open and leave 15 minutes to dry and crisp.

To prepare for serving, cut each éclair in half lengthwise. With a sharp knife gently scoop out and discard any moist pastry. Fill bottom halves with your favorite fruit pudding or whipped cream topping and cover with pastry tops. Spoon additional whipped cream over the tops, or cover with a strip of jam. Yields 8 éclairs.

POPOVERS

Delicate, light, and golden.

Pastry:

3 eggs

½ cup milk

1 tablespoon vegetable oil

1¼ cups unbleached white flour

Filling:

3 cups filling (see recommendations below)

Place a muffin pan in a 425 degree oven to heat while preparing popovers. In a medium-sized mixing bowl combine eggs, milk, and oil and blend well. Add flour and beat thoroughly. Remove heated muffin pan from oven and grease generously and quickly. Fill muffin wells half full of batter and return to the oven. Bake 15 minutes or until firm to the touch and lightly browned. Best served immediately, but may be cooled on a wire rack and served later. (If you prefer crispy popovers, after removing them from the oven slit the side of each with a sharp knife to allow steam to escape. Return to turned-off oven with door slightly open and allow popovers to dry 20 minutes.)

To serve, fill popovers with your favorite fruit pudding, custard, ice cream, sherbet, cottage cheese and fresh fruit, meringue, yogurt, or well-drained canned fruit. Top, if you wish, with blended fruit, whipped cream, flaked coconut, ice cream, fruit gel, or nuts. (See Toppings, pages 127–131.) Yields 9 popovers.

DESSERT CRÊPES

An elegant dessert filled with fruit, pudding, or creams.

Crêpes:

2 eggs, beaten

1 cup milk

1 cup unbleached white flour

¼ teaspoon cinnamon

Filling:

Sliced fresh fruit or any filling suggested below.

Stir crêpe ingredients together in a medium-sized bowl. Cover and allow to stand ½ hour. Heat and oil a 6″ frying pan. Pour in just enough batter to cover the bottom and tilt pan to form round crêpe. Turn when lightly browned and cook the other side. Remove from heat. Stack finished crêpes on a plate and cover with a linen towel.

To serve, fill warm crêpes with your choice of fresh fruit, fruit pudding, whipped cream topping, jam, spread, or fruit butter. (See index for recipes.) Top, if you wish, with ice cream, sherbet, meringue, or whipped cream. Serves 10 (2 crêpes each).

FANCY FRUIT TURNOVERS

Sweet fruit filling in flaky pastry.

Pastry:
2 cups unbleached white flour
⅔ cup butter, softened
6 or 7 tablespoons water

⅓ cup butter

Filling:
2½ cups fruit filling (see recommendations below)

Measure flour and ⅔ cup softened butter into a mixing bowl; mix well with a fork or pastry blender until mixture resembles coarse meal. Gradually add water, using just enough to form a soft dough. Roll out on a lightly floured surface to ⅛″ thickness. Slice off bits of ⅓ cup butter with a sharp knife and place on rolled-out pastry so that pastry is covered fairly evenly with specks of butter. Fold top of pastry down to the center, bottom up to center, and sides into the center. Wrap in plastic and chill well.

To prepare turnovers, place pastry on a lightly floured surface and roll out to ⅛″ thickness. With a sharp knife cut into 4″ squares. Place ¼ cup filling in the center of each. Wet the edges of the pastry with milk, fold over into triangles, and crimp the edges securely together with the tines of a fork. Cut a slit in the top to allow steam to escape. Place turnovers on oiled baking sheets. Bake at 425 degrees for 15 to 20 minutes or until browned. Cool on wire racks and serve warm or chilled. Yields 10 turnovers.

• Fillings
Apple Turnovers—Fill each with chopped apple, raisins, nutmeg, and cinnamon.

Blueberry Turnovers—Fill each with blueberries.

Peach Turnovers—Fill each with chopped peach, dash of cinnamon.

Pear Turnovers—Fill each with chopped pear, dash of nutmeg, ground walnuts.

Plum Turnovers—Fill each with chopped plum.

Pineapple Turnovers—Fill each with chopped pineapple, dash of cinnamon.

Pies and Tarts

Pies

Filled with tender fruit, custard, or pudding, a homemade pie is an all-American dessert. Apples, pears, pineapples, bananas, and peaches all make deliciously sweet pies bubbling with natural juices. Sprinkle with spices, nuts, and crumb toppings; adorn in fancy lattice crusts; or serve warm with melted cheese. Bake an extra to freeze and serve as a warm, wholesome dessert on a cold winter evening.

Helpful Hints

1. Prepare pie crust as directed.
2. Bake in 9″ round pie pan unless otherwise indicated.
3. Lightly oil pie pans.
4. Generously fill pie shells with washed, peeled, cored, sliced, fresh fruit.

5. To prebake pie shells, prick rolled-out pastry with a fork and bake as directed.

6. To seal top and bottom crusts, sprinkle milk over bottom crust rim, cover pie with top crust, and press firmly together with any of the recommended edgings (see Pretty Pie Crusts).

7. Always slit the top crust before baking to allow the steam to escape.

8. To fill custard pies, pull the oven rack out to full extension, place the empty pie shell on it, carefully pour in the custard filling, and gently slide the pie and rack into the oven. This helps to avoid spills from carrying full pie from counter to oven.

9. Crumb crust toppings are excellent and easy top crusts for fruit pies.

10. Bake fruit pies just until fruit is tender. Do not overbake.

11. When custard pie has set, the top is lightly brown and creased around the edges. The pie jiggles as one mass when gently shaken. And most reliably, a knife inserted in the center comes out clean. Avoid overcooking custards.

12. Serve warm or cooled. Store refrigerated.

13. Fresh fruit pies freeze well; wrap securely in aluminum foil. Do not freeze custard or pudding pies.

Recipe Suggestions

Flour Substitutions—Refer to Fortify with Flour (see pages 140–142) for recommended flours, substitution guidelines, and suggested amounts.

Pie Mix-In and Bake-On—Try the following suggestions to perk up your pies.

1. *Bottom*—Before adding the pie filling, line the bottom crust with any of the following: jam, nut butter, chopped nuts, seeds, flaked coconut, wheat germ, fresh fruit slices, nutmeg, cinnamon, ginger, or one of the Sprinkle-On Toppings (see pages 127–128). Fill pie shell and bake as directed.

2. *Middle*—Any of the following may be stirred into pudding or fresh fruit pie fillings before spooning into pastry-lined pie pan: chopped nuts, seeds, raisins, granola, roasted soybeans, toasted wheat germ, chopped dried fruit, grated cheese, flaked coconut, chopped fresh fruit, grated carrot, toasted rolled oats, or a Sprinkle-On Topping (see pages 127–128).

3. *Top*—Add the following for quick and easy pie toppings: flaked coconut, chopped nuts, seeds, fruit pudding, yogurt, spices, chopped dried fruit, whole berries, ice cream, sherbet, sliced fresh fruit, or a Spoon-On Topping (see pages 129–130).

Pretty Pie Crusts

Try the following suggestions with rolled-out pastries to produce attractive pie crusts.

• Using Bottom Crust

Fluted—Use your fingers to press from opposite directions to produce zigzag edges.

Tined—Use the tines of a fork to press firmly around edge of crust.

Waved—Add a strip of pastry ½" wide to crust edge in a wavy pattern, securing firmly to crust.

Scalloped—Use a round spoon and press against your fingers with crust in between to produce rounded edges.

• Using Bottom and Top Crust

Lattice—Use ½" wide strips of rolled-out pastry. Weave in a lattice pattern, set half the strips in one direction and then cross them with remaining strips, or twist strips as you place them on pie.

Free-flow—Cut patterns or designs out of rolled pastry and arrange over filling.

Carved Crust—With a small sharp knife carve patterns or designs into top crust.

Fancy Edges—Secure top crust to bottom as suggested for bottom crust (see above).

NEW ENGLAND APPLE PIE

A spicy apple and raisin pie in a flaky butter pastry.

Pastry:
2 cups unbleached white flour
⅔ cup butter, softened
6 or 7 tablespoons water

Filling:
¾ cup raisins
¾ cup water

7 or 8 cooking apples (6 cups peeled, cored, and sliced)
1 tablespoon lemon juice
2 tablespoons unbleached white flour
1 teaspoon cinnamon
½ teaspoon nutmeg
Dash each of ginger and ground cloves

Measure flour and butter into a small mixing bowl and mix well. Add water gradually, using just enough to form a soft dough. Divide dough in half, roll each half into a ball, flatten, and roll out on floured surface to ⅛" thickness. Fit one pastry circle into 9" pie pan and reserve remaining pastry to cover filling.

In a small saucepan combine raisins with ¾ cup water and bring to a boil. Remove from heat and allow to stand, covered, 10 minutes to soften. Drain off excess water and combine raisins with sliced apples, lemon juice, flour, and spices. Toss well. Pour into pastry-lined pie pan and mound up the filling in the center. Cover with reserved pastry. Crimp edges securely together and slit the top to allow steam to escape. Bake at 350 degrees for 40 minutes or until crust is browned and fruit is tender. Serve chilled, or warm with a slice of cheddar cheese. Serves 8.

BANANA COCONUT CUSTARD PIE

Filling whips up easily in a blender.

Pastry:
½ cup unbleached white flour
1 cup rolled oats
¾ cup flaked coconut
5 tablespoons vegetable oil
¼ teaspoon nutmeg
Unsweetened fruit juice

Filling:
1½ cups milk
3 eggs
2 ripe bananas, cut in pieces
1 teaspoon nutmeg
½ teaspoon baking powder
⅓ cup unbleached white flour
1 cup flaked coconut

Topping:
½ cup flaked coconut
1 ripe banana, sliced

In a medium-sized mixing bowl combine pastry ingredients except fruit juice; mix well. Gradually add fruit juice, using just enough to form a soft dough. Press pastry into lightly oiled 9" pie pan, covering bottom and sides evenly.

Combine filling ingredients in a blender and blend well. Pour into pastry-lined pie pan. Sprinkle liberally with nutmeg. Bake at 350 degrees for 50 minutes or until custard has set. Cool and refrigerate.

Shortly before serving, sprinkle pie with ½ cup flaked coconut and garnish with banana slices. Serve immediately. Serves 8.

NATURAL BLUEBERRY PIE

A delicious, mildly tart pie.

Pastry:
2 cups unbleached white flour
⅔ cup butter, softened
6 or 7 tablespoons water

Filling:
4½ cups fresh blueberries
1 tablespoon unsweetened pineapple
   juice concentrate
⅓ cup unbleached white flour

To make pastry, measure flour and butter into a mixing bowl. Mix with a fork until crumbly. Add water gradually, using just enough to form a soft, pliable dough. Divide into two portions. Roll each half into a ball and flatten. Roll each out on a floured surface to ⅛" thickness. Fit bottom crust into 9″ pie pan and reserve remaining pastry sheet for top crust.

Wash and pick over blueberries, discarding any that are damaged. Toss blueberries in a large mixing bowl with concentrated pineapple juice. Toss with flour. Pour into pastry-lined pie pan and cover with remaining sheet of pastry. Slit the top. Bake at 450 degrees for 10 minutes, reduce heat to 350 degrees, and continue baking for 30 minutes more. Cool, and serve warm or chilled, topped with ice cream, whipped cream, or fruit pudding if you desire. Serves 8.

GRANOLA FRUIT PIE

Made with fresh fruit in season.

Pastry and Topping:

2 cups granola (flaked coconut, chopped nuts, dried fruit, rolled oats, seeds, and/or spices)

2 cups unbleached white flour

½ cup vegetable oil

Unsweetened fruit juice

Filling:

4 or 5 cups mixed, sliced, fresh fruit (apple, pear, peach, pineapple, rhubarb, whole blueberries, etc.)

¼ cup unbleached white flour

1 tablespoon lemon juice

Cinnamon and nutmeg to taste

In a medium-sized mixing bowl combine granola, flour, and oil and mix well. Gradually add fruit juice, adding just enough to form a soft dough. Divide mixture in half. Press one portion into a lightly oiled 9″ pie pan, covering bottom and sides evenly. Save the remaining half for the topping.

In a large bowl toss fresh fruit with flour, lemon juice, and spices to taste. Spoon into pastry-lined pie pan and sprinkle evenly with reserved granola topping. Bake at 375 degrees for 40 minutes or until fruit is tender. Cool and refrigerate.

To serve, top each slice with chopped fresh fruit. Serves 8.

CINNAMON PEACH PIE

A delicious pie packed with fresh peach slices and laced with spice.

Pastry:
2 cups unbleached white flour
¼ cup vegetable oil
6 or 7 tablespoons water

Filling:
5 cups sliced fresh peaches
¼ cup unbleached white flour
1 teaspoon lemon juice
2 teaspoons cinnamon

Topping:
1 pint heavy cream
1 teaspoon vanilla extract
1 fresh peach, sliced

In a medium-sized bowl combine flour and oil for pastry. Mix until crumbly. Gradually add water, using just enough to form a soft, pliable dough. Divide in half, roll each half into a ball, flatten, and roll each out on floured surface to ⅛″ thickness. Fit one pastry circle into 9″ pie pan and reserve remaining pastry for top crust.

Combine sliced peaches with flour, lemon juice, and cinnamon; toss in a large bowl. Spoon into pastry-lined pie pan and cover with remaining sheet of pastry. Secure pastry edges together by fluting or crimping crust. Slit the top crust to allow steam to escape, and bake in preheated oven at 425 degrees for 15 minutes; reduce heat to 350 degrees and continue baking for 25 minutes more. Cool and refrigerate.

Shortly before serving, whip heavy cream and vanilla just until fluffy. Do not overbeat. Spoon whipped cream over pie and garnish with sliced fresh peach. Serve immediately. Serves 8.

SUMMER PEAR PIE

Light, sweet pears in a crunchy pie shell. A family favorite.

Pastry and Topping:
1½ cups unbleached white flour
2 cups rolled oats
½ cup vegetable oil
½ to ⅔ cup unsweetened fruit juice

Filling:
7 or 8 fresh pears, peeled and sliced
1 tablespoon lemon juice
2 tablespoons unbleached white flour
1 teaspoon nutmeg

Combine flour, rolled oats, and oil in a medium-sized bowl and mix well; add just enough juice to form a soft dough. Spoon half of this mixture into a lightly oiled 9″ pie pan and press evenly over bottom and sides. Reserve remaining half for topping.

In a large mixing bowl combine sliced pears with lemon juice, flour, and nutmeg; toss well. Spoon into pastry-lined pie pan and sprinkle evenly with crumb pastry reserved for topping. Bake at 375 degrees for 45 minutes or until pears are tender when tested by knife inserted in the center. Cool on wire rack.

Serve slightly warm or cooled. Try serving with a scoop of fruit-sweetened ice cream or sherbet. Serves 8.

PINEAPPLE CREAM CUSTARD PIE

A golden vanilla-pineapple pie smothered with rich whipped cream.

Pastry:
1 cup unbleached white flour
⅛ cup vegetable oil
3 to 4 tablespoons water

Filling:
one 20-oz. can crushed pineapple in unsweetened juice

1½ cups milk
3 eggs
1 teaspoon vanilla extract

Topping:
1 pint heavy cream
1 teaspoon vanilla extract
½ cup crushed pineapple, well drained (reserved from filling)

Combine flour and oil in a small mixing bowl. Gradually add water, using just enough to form a soft dough. Shape into a ball, flatten, and roll out on floured surface to ⅛″ thickness. Line a 9″ pie pan with pastry.

Pour the canned pineapple and juice into a bowl. Measure out ½ cup pineapple pieces to reserve for topping. Pour the remainder into a food processor or blender and whip until creamy and smooth. Add milk, eggs, and vanilla to mixture and blend well. Pour into pastry-lined pie pan and bake in preheated oven at 350 degrees for one hour or until custard has set. Cool and refrigerate.

Shortly before serving, whip heavy cream and vanilla in a small mixing bowl just until light and fluffy. Do not overbeat. Mix in well-drained crushed pineapple and spoon over pie. Serves 8.

FANCY PINEAPPLE LATTICE PIE

A sweet, spicy pie in an attractive woven crust. A festive company dish.

Pastry:
2 cups unbleached white flour
⅔ cup butter, softened
½ teaspoon almond extract
6 or 7 tablespoons water

Filling:
1 fresh pineapple (four cups chopped)
¼ cup unbleached white flour
1 teaspoon lemon juice
½ teaspoon nutmeg
1 teaspoon cinnamon
¾ cup chopped walnuts

In a small mixing bowl work together flour and butter for pastry. Add almond extract and mix. Gradually add water, using just enough to form a soft dough. Divide in half, roll each half into a ball, flatten, and roll each out on floured surface to ⅛" thickness. Fit one piece into 9" pie pan and reserve the remainder for the lattice crust.

Slice and chop fresh pineapple. In a large mixing bowl toss pineapple with flour, lemon juice, and spices. Spoon into pastry-lined pie pan and sprinkle with chopped nuts. Slice remaining pastry sheet in ½" strips. Lay strips in one direction over pie filling, leaving ½" between strips. Repeat process, laying strips across original ones. Twist the strips as you place them, or weave them over and under for a fancier lattice topping. Flute pie edges, securing strips to pie bottom crust. Bake at 425 degrees for 25 to 30 minutes or until crust is nicely browned. Cool and refrigerate.

To serve, top with a scoop of Pineapple Sherbet (page 115). Serves 8.

OLD-FASHIONED PUMPKIN PIE

A creamy pumpkin custard pie in a delicious walnut crust.

Pastry:
1 cup unbleached white flour
1 cup ground walnuts (whirl nuts in
   a blender or food processor)
3 tablespoons vegetable oil
¼ cup unsweetened fruit juice or
   water

Filling:
2 cups pumpkin (cooked, drained,
   and mashed)
1 cup milk
1 teaspoon vanilla extract
1 teaspoon nutmeg
1 teaspoon cinnamon
⅛ teaspoon ginger
⅛ teaspoon cloves
3 egg yolks

Combine pastry ingredients and mix well. Press evenly into a lightly oiled 9″ pie pan.

Combine filling ingredients in a blender and blend well. Pour into pastry-lined pie pan and sprinkle liberally with additional nutmeg. Bake at 350 degrees for 40 minutes or until custard has set. Cool on wire rack and refrigerate. Delicious plain or topped with whipped cream. Serves 8.

PUMPKIN CHEESECAKE PIE

An elegant, unusual pie.

Pastry:
¾ cup unbleached white flour
1 cup rolled oats
¼ cup vegetable oil
¼ teaspoon almond extract
¼ to ⅓ cup unsweetened fruit juice

Filling:
1½ cups cottage cheese
1½ cups pumpkin (cooked, drained,

and mashed)
3 eggs
1 teaspoon nutmeg
1 teaspoon cinnamon
3 tablespoons unbleached white
flour

Topping:
1 pint heavy cream
1 teaspoon vanilla extract

To make pastry, combine flour, rolled oats, oil, and almond extract until well blended. Gradually add fruit juice, adding just enough to form a soft dough. Press dough evenly in lightly oiled 9" pie pan.

Combine all the filling ingredients in a blender and blend well. Pour into pastry-lined pie pan. Bake at 350 degrees for 50 minutes or until custard has set. Cool and refrigerate.

Shortly before serving, whip heavy cream and vanilla extract together in a small bowl until light and fluffy. Do not overbeat. Spoon over pie and serve. Serves 8.

Tarts

An old-fashioned, special dessert, tarts can be made with a wide variety of mouth-watering fillings and fancy toppings.

Pastry—Any of the pie crust pastries may be prepared for use in tart shells. Use a roll-out recipe (yields two crusts) or double a crumb crust recipe.

Preparation—Gently press pastry into standard tart shells and pre-bake as directed, or fill with filling and bake as directed.

Muffin Pan Tart Shells—To make your own tart shells, start with a muffin pan having 1½" round by ¾" deep muffin wells. Prepare pastry as directed. Either grease the inside of the muffin wells and press in roll-out or crumb pastry to form tarts or invert the muffin pans, grease the outsides of the muffin wells, and place roll-out pastry over wells to form tarts. Bake as directed, cool, and fill with filling. If the filling is to be baked with the tart shell, use the first method.

Baked Filling—Delicious fillings that bake with the tart shells include a wide variety of custard recipes. Also, recipes for fresh fruit pies may be easily adapted to tarts. Simply fill each tart with a small portion of the fruit pie filling, cover with a crumb crust or pastry topping, and bake as directed.

Non-baked fillings—All the fruit sauce puddings make excellent tart fillings. Jams, sherbets, ice creams, fresh fruit, whipped cream, yogurt, meringue, and cheese mixtures make fine fillings. See Spoon-On Toppings (pages 129–130).

Toppings and Garnishes—Cinnamon, nutmeg, jam, seeds, coconut, fresh fruit pieces, and nuts are simple and appealing garnishes. Often a fresh whole berry or nut piece is all that is required to adorn this elegant dessert. The numerous toppings suggested for pies are also suitable for tarts.

APPLESAUCE CUSTARD TARTS

Sweet, light custard in flaky butter pastry.

Pastry:
1 cup unbleached white flour
⅓ cup butter, softened
3 to 4 tablespoons water or unsweetened apple juice

Filling:
¾ cup unsweetened applesauce
½ cup milk

2 eggs
½ teaspoon cinnamon

Topping:
Unsweetened applesauce
1 apple, sliced

To prepare pastry, combine flour and butter. Gradually add just enough water or fruit juice to form a soft dough. Pinch off pieces and press into lightly oiled tart pans or small muffin wells. Line each tin evenly with pastry.

Combine filling ingredients in a blender and blend well. Pour into pastry-lined tart pans and sprinkle with cinnamon. Bake in preheated oven at 425 degrees for 10 minutes, reduce heat to 350 degrees, and continue baking 20 to 25 minutes more or until custard has set. Cool and refrigerate.

To serve, top each tart with a spoonful of applesauce and a slice of fresh apple. Yields 12 to 14 tarts.

BANANA CLOUD TARTS

A smooth pudding with whipped carob topping.

Pastry:
1 cup rolled oats
½ cup unbleached white flour
¾ cup flaked coconut
5 tablespoons vegetable oil
¼ teaspoon nutmeg
Unsweetened fruit juice

Filling:
2¼ cups blended banana (whip
    chopped banana in a blender or
    food processor)
3 tablespoons cornstarch

Topping:
½ pint heavy cream
½ teaspoon vanilla extract
3 tablespoons carob powder

In a medium-sized mixing bowl combine pastry ingredients except fruit juice and mix well. Gradually add fruit juice, using just enough to form a soft dough. Pinch off pieces of pastry and press into oiled tart tins. Bake in preheated oven at 375 degrees for 15 minutes or until lightly browned. Cool and remove tarts from tins.

Combine blended banana and cornstarch in a blender; mix well. Pour into the top of a double boiler set over the bottom filled with hot water. Heat over medium setting. Stir constantly as mixture reaches a boil and thickens. Remove from heat and cool. Spoon into prebaked tart shells and refrigerate.

Shortly before serving, beat together heavy cream, vanilla extract, and carob powder in a small bowl at high speed. Beat just until mixture reaches a light and fluffy consistency. Do not overbeat. Spoon generously over tarts and serve immediately. Yields 12 to 14 tarts.

PEACHY DREAM TARTS

Delightful peach flavor in nutty tart shells.

Pastry:
1 cup unbleached white flour
1 cup ground pecans (chop nuts in a
　food processor or blender)
3 tablespoons vegetable oil
¼ cup unsweetened fruit juice (ap-
　proximately)

Filling:
2¼ cups blended peaches (blend
　chopped fresh or canned peaches
　in a blender or food processor)
3 tablespoons cornstarch

Topping:
⅓ cup flaked coconut
12 to 14 pecan halves

Combine crust ingredients, adding just enough fruit juice to form a soft dough. Press into oiled tart pans. Bake at 375 degrees for 15 to 20 minutes or until lightly browned. Cool and remove from tins.

Combine blended peaches and cornstarch in a blender and whip until smooth. Pour into the top of a double boiler set over the bottom filled with hot water, and heat over medium setting. Stir constantly as mixture reaches a boil and thickens. Remove from heat and cool. Spoon into prebaked tart shells.

Top each tart with a sprinkle of flaked coconut and a pecan half. Store refrigerated until serving. Yields 12 to 14 tarts.

CREAMY PEAR TARTS

Easy and delicious. A welcome change from traditional tarts.

Pastry:
¾ cup unbleached white flour
1 cup rolled oats
¼ cup vegetable oil
¼ to ⅓ cup unsweetened pear juice

Filling:
¾ cup blended pear (whip chopped
　fresh or canned pear in a blender
　or food processor)

½ cup milk
2 eggs
¼ teaspoon nutmeg

Topping:
Chopped dates

To prepare pastry, combine flour, oats, and oil and mix well. Add just enough pear juice to form a soft dough. Press dough evenly into oiled tart pans or small muffin wells.

Combine filling ingredients in a blender and blend well. Spoon filling into pastry-lined tart pans and sprinkle with additional nutmeg. Bake at 425 degrees for 10 minutes, reduce heat to 350 degrees, and continue baking 20 to 25 minutes or until custard has set. Cool and refrigerate.

Top each chilled tart with chopped dates and serve. Yields 12 to 14 tarts.

Fruit Breads

Filled with fresh fruit and nuts, these simple breads can be served plain, frosted, or smothered with pudding and cream, fruit sauce, fresh fruit, or ice cream. Fruit breads are a versatile, easy-to-prepare dessert, and go well with any meal. Serve sliced at breakfast, lightly toasted if you prefer, and spread with jam or butter. Make sandwiches with fruit bread for lunch or serve sliced in a bread basket with dinner. Delicious with afternoon tea or as a wholesome after-school snack for the kids, these breads are a versatile addition to anyone's table.

Helpful Hints

1. The following recipes require a 9″ by 5″ loaf pan.
2. Generously grease and flour pans.
3. When cooking thick batters, spread batter evenly in the pan before baking.
4. When bread is done it will be browned, pulled slightly away from the sides of the pan, and a knife inserted will come out clean.

5. Allow breads to cool briefly in the pan before turning out on racks to cool.
6. Cool breads completely before storing.
7. Fruit breads freeze well. Wrap securely in aluminum foil.

Recipe Suggestions

Flour Substitutions—Refer to Fortify with Flour (see pages 140–142) for recommended flours, substitution guidelines, and suggested amounts.

Fruit Bread Mix-In—Stir any of the following into the batter before baking for variety, flavor, and texture: chopped nuts, seeds, jam, sliced fresh fruit, spices, carob chips, granola, nut butter, grated carrot, whole berries, chopped dates, raisins, herbs, or flaked coconut.

Fruit Bread Bake-On—Sprinkle any of the following over batter before baking for exciting and delicious toppings. If batter is thick, gently press topping into batter with the back of a spoon. Topping suggestions include nuts, spices, flaked coconut, rolled oats, wheat germ, bits of jam, sliced fruit, nut butter, or your favorite Sprinkle-On Topping (see pages 127–128).

Fruit Bread Toppings—Allow bread to cool and frost generously with any of the following: jam, cream cheese, nut butter, seed butter, or a Spread-On Topping (see page 129).

Fruit Bread Spoon-On Topping—Place a generous slice of fruit bread on a dessert plate. Spoon on yogurt, fruit sauce, fruit pudding, ice cream, sherbet, or any Spoon-On Topping (see pages 129–130). Serve immediately.

APRICOT BREAD

A sweet loaf filled with bits of dried apricots.

2 large eggs

1/3 cup mashed banana (mash ripe banana with a fork)

2/3 cup water

2 teaspoons vanilla extract

1/3 cup vegetable oil

2 cups unbleached white flour

1 teaspoon baking soda

2 teaspoons baking powder

2 cups finely chopped dried apricots (see note below)

Beat together eggs and mashed banana until creamy. Add water, vanilla extract, and oil and beat. Measure in flour, baking soda, and baking powder. Beat well. Stir in chopped apricot until evenly blended. Spoon batter into an oiled and floured 9" by 5" loaf pan. Spread batter evenly in pan. Bake at 325 degrees for 45 minutes or until a knife inserted comes out clean. Cool completely on a wire rack before slicing. Serves 6.

• Note

Apricots must be cut into small pieces so that they will disperse evenly in the batter. If you mix in large pieces, they will sink to the bottom of the pan during baking.

HOME-STYLE BANANA BREAD

Banana bread is a welcome addition to any meal.

3/4 cup mashed banana (mash ripe banana with a fork)

1/3 cup vegetable oil

2 large eggs

1/2 cup water

2 cups unbleached white flour

1 teaspoon baking soda

2 teaspoons baking powder

1/2 teaspoon cinnamon

1/2 teaspoon nutmeg

1 cup chopped walnuts

Beat together mashed banana, oil, eggs, and water until creamy. Add flour, baking soda, baking powder, and spices. Beat well. Stir in chopped walnuts. Spoon batter into an oiled and floured 9" by 5" loaf pan. Spread batter evenly in pan. Bake at 325 degrees for 45 minutes or until a knife inserted comes out clean. Cool completely on a wire rack before slicing. Serves 6.

CINNAMON ORANGE BREAD

Moist, light, and spicy. Great for gingerbread lovers.

Bread:
3 large eggs
½ cup butter, softened
1 cup unsweetened orange juice
2½ cups unbleached white flour
1 teaspoon baking soda

1 teaspoon baking powder
2 teaspoons cinnamon
¾ cup chopped nuts

Topping:
½ pint heavy cream
½ teaspoon orange extract

Beat together eggs, butter, and juice. Add flour, baking soda, baking powder, and cinnamon; mix well. Stir in chopped nuts. Spoon into oiled and floured 9″ by 5″ loaf pan. Spread evenly in pan. Bake at 325 degrees for 55 minutes or until browned and a knife inserted in the center comes out clean. Cool on wire rack.

To prepare topping, beat together heavy cream and orange extract just until light and fluffy. Spoon over warm Cinnamon Orange Bread slices and serve. Serves 6.

CRANBERRY APPLE BREAD

Light apple loaf with cranberries and chopped apple throughout.

Bread:
¾ cup unsweetened applesauce
⅓ cup vegetable oil
2 large eggs
¼ cup water
2 cups unbleached white flour
1 teaspoon baking soda
2 teaspoons baking powder
½ teaspoon nutmeg

1 teaspoon cinnamon
1 chopped fresh apple (peel, core, and chop in approximately ⅓″ cubes)
½ cup chopped fresh cranberries

Topping:
1 8-oz. package cream cheese, softened

In a mixing bowl beat together applesauce, oil, eggs, and water. Add flour, baking soda, baking powder, and spices. Beat well. Stir in chopped apple and cranberries. Spoon batter into an oiled and floured 9″ by 5″ loaf pan. Spread batter evenly in pan. Bake at 325 degrees for 40 to 45 minutes or until a knife inserted in the center comes out clean. Cool on a wire rack. Serve plain or top each slice with softened cream cheese. Serves 6.

TANGY LEMON LOAF

Lemon flavor with a hint of spice. Nice change from very sweet desserts.

Loaf:

¼ cup unsweetened pineapple juice

¾ cup blended pineapple (whip un-
　sweetened canned pineapple, in-
　cluding juice, in a food processor
　or blender until smooth)

½ teaspoon lemon extract

2 large eggs

⅓ cup vegetable oil

2 cups unbleached white flour

1 teaspoon baking soda

2 teaspoons baking powder

½ teaspoon cinnamon

½ teaspoon grated lemon peel

¾ cup chopped walnuts

In a mixing bowl beat together pineapple juice, blended pineapple, lemon extract, eggs, and oil. Add flour, baking soda, baking powder, cinnamon, and lemon peel and beat well. Stir in chopped walnuts. Spoon batter into an oiled and floured 9" by 5" loaf pan. Spread batter evenly in pan. Bake at 325 degrees for 30 to 40 minutes or until a knife inserted in the center comes out clean. Cool on wire rack. Serves 6.

MOIST AND RICH CAROB BREAD

An unusually rich and delicious bread.

Bread:

½ cup carob powder

2 large eggs

¾ cup mashed banana (mash ripe
　banana with a fork)

½ cup water

⅓ cup vegetable oil

2 teaspoons vanilla extract

1¾ cups unbleached white flour

2 teaspoons baking powder

1 teaspoon baking soda

1 cup chopped walnuts

Topping:

1 3-oz. package cream cheese

In a mixing bowl beat together carob powder, eggs, and mashed banana. Add water, oil, and vanilla extract and beat. Measure in flour, baking powder, and baking soda. Beat well. Stir in chopped walnuts. Spoon batter into an oiled and floured 9" by 5" loaf pan. Spread batter evenly in pan. Bake at 325 degrees for 45 minutes or until a knife inserted in the center comes out clean. Cool loaf on a wire rack before slicing. Serves 6.

ORANGE CRUMB BREAD

Orange-flavored bread with a center of spice and nuts.

Bread:

⅓ cup vegetable oil

2 large eggs

⅓ cup mashed banana (mash ripe banana with a fork)

⅔ cup unsweetened orange juice

½ teaspoon orange extract

2 cups unbleached white flour

1 teaspoon baking soda

2 teaspoons baking powder

Topping:

½ cup chopped walnuts

½ teaspoon cinnamon

½ teaspoon nutmeg

In a medium-sized mixing bowl beat together oil, eggs, mashed banana, orange juice, and orange extract until well blended. Add flour, baking soda, and baking powder. Beat well. Spoon half of the batter evenly into an oiled and floured 9" by 5" loaf pan. Sprinkle with half of the topping, smooth on the remaining batter, and sprinkle over it the remaining topping. Bake at 325 degrees for 40 minutes or until loaf is nicely browned and a knife inserted comes out clean. Cool on a wire rack. Loaf cuts best when completely cooled. Serves 6.

RAISIN BREAD

Wonderful for breakfast.

Bread:

2 large eggs

¼ cup water

¾ cup blended pear (whip chopped fresh or canned pear in a food processor or blender until smooth)

⅓ cup vegetable oil

2 cups unbleached white flour

2 teaspoons baking powder

1 teaspoon baking soda

½ teaspoon nutmeg

1½ cups raisins

Beat together in a medium-sized bowl eggs, water, blended pear, and oil until creamy. Add flour, baking powder, baking soda, and nutmeg. Beat well. Stir in raisins. Spoon batter into an oiled and floured 9" by 5" loaf pan. Spread batter evenly in pan. Bake at 325 degrees for 45 minutes or until a knife inserted in the center comes out clean. Cool completely on a wire rack before slicing. Serves 6.

Compotes, Crisps, and Upside-Down Cakes

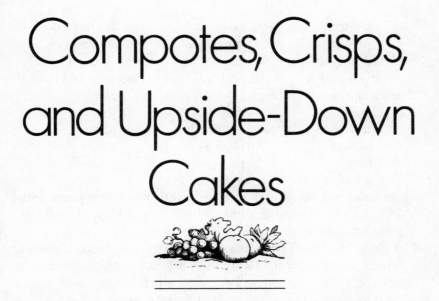

These compotes, crisps, upside-down cakes, and fruit casseroles are moist, fragrant blends of the delicious flavors and textures fruit has to offer. Serve a warm fruit compote with breakfast on a cold winter morning. And what could be easier to whip up for unexpected guests than a banana crisp?

Recipe Suggestions

Recommended Fruits to Boil—Simmer in liquid, covered, on the stove until tender.

apple	dried fruit	plum
apricot	peach	prune
banana	pear	rhubarb
berries	pineapple	

Recommended Fruits to Broil—Place fruit on baking sheets or in casserole dishes and broil in the oven until warm and tender.

apple	berries	guava
banana	grapefruit	mango

orange	pear	prune
papaya	pineapple	tangerine
peach	plum	

Recommended Fruits to Bake—Place fruit in casseroles and bake at moderate heat (350 degrees) until warm and tender.

apple	grapefruit	pear
apricot	mango	plum
banana	orange	pineapple
berries	papaya	prune
guava	peach	

Flour Substitutions—Refer to Fortify with Flour (see pages 140–142) for recommended flours, substitution guidelines, and suggested amounts.

Hot Fruit Mix-In—Try mixing the following into fruit casseroles, broiled, or boiled fruits for exciting flavors and texture combinations: chopped nuts, flaked coconut, wheat germ, seeds, rolled oats, spices, another chopped fresh fruit, chopped dried fruit, or herbs.

Hot Fruit Bake-On—Sprinkle the following over baked or broiled fruits. If desired, crisp under the broiler for a few minutes to lightly brown and warm topping. Suggestions include flaked coconut, nuts, seeds, wheat germ, chopped dried fruit, chopped fresh fruit, roasted soybeans, or Sprinkle-On Toppings (See pages 127–128).

Hot Fruit Spoon-On Toppings—Any of the following are delicious spooned over baked, broiled, or stewed fruits: yogurt, sherbet, ice cream, fruit sauce, fruit pudding, or a Spoon-On Topping (see pages 129–130). Serve immediately.

BAKED WHOLE FRUIT

Warm, soft fruit with a sweet filling.
6 fresh apples, pears, or peaches
Fruit filling (see recommendations below)
    Wash fruit. Peel off the top ¼ of the skin. With a small sharp knife gently core the fruit without cutting through the bottom.

Wrap each fruit loosely ¾ of the way up with foil to retain juices. Spoon in filling and bake as directed. Serve warm and top with pudding, meringue, or whipped cream. Serves 6.

Baked Apples—at 350 degrees for 45 minutes or until tender.

Baked Peaches—at 350 degrees for 20 minutes or until tender.

Baked Pears—at 350 degrees for 20 minutes or until tender.

• Recommended Fruit Fillings

Chopped dates, nuts, and a dash of nutmeg; chunks of well-drained fresh fruit; nuts and canned fruit; mashed fresh fruit; any dried fruit combination.

BROILED FRUIT WEDGES

Warm, sweet, and simple.

4 whole fresh fruit (see recommenda-   *Lemon juice*
tions below)   *Nutmeg and cinnamon*

Wash, core, peel, and slice fruit into wedges or chunks. Toss with lemon juice and spices to taste. Broil on oiled baking sheet until fruit is tender.

Serve warm, topped with ice cream, sherbet, whipped cream, or fruit pudding. Serves 6.

• Recommended Fruits

Apples, bananas, orange halves (in rind), peaches, pears, pineapple.

FRUIT BAKE

A hearty and delicious warm fruit dessert. Substitute different fruit if you wish.

4 teaspoons unbleached white flour   *½ cup flaked coconut or chopped*
1 tablespoon cold water   *nuts*
1 20-oz. can crushed pineapple in   *½ teaspoon nutmeg*
unsweetened juice   *1 tablespoon bread crumbs or wheat*
3 bananas   *germ*
1 teaspoon lemon juice

Mix flour and water in a small bowl. Combine with pineapple (including juice) and bring to a boil over medium heat. Stir often as mixture thickens. Remove from heat and set aside. Oil a 9″ square baking casserole and line with bananas, peeled and cut into ½″ slices. Sprinkle with lemon juice, coconut or nuts, and nutmeg. Pour hot pineapple mixture evenly over all and sprinkle with bread crumbs. Bake at 350 degrees for 15 minutes.

Serve warm, plain or topped with whipped cream, homemade ice cream, or yogurt. Serves 6.

HOT FRUIT COMPOTE

Warm fruit in spicy sauce.

4 cups chopped fresh fruit	*Unsweetened fruit juice*
(see recommendations below)	*Nutmeg and cinnamon*

In a medium-sized saucepan place chopped fresh fruit and add just enough fruit juice to cover fruit. Sprinkle with nutmeg and cinnamon to taste. Heat over low heat, stirring occasionally, until fruit is tender.

Serve warm in dessert bowls. Serves 4 to 6.

• Recommended Fruits

Apples, bananas, whole blueberries, peaches, pears, pineapple.

BROILED BANANA CRISP

Quick and easy. Substitute fresh fruits in season.

4 small ripe bananas	*2 tablespoons flour*
1 tablespoon lemon juice	*¼ teaspoon cinnamon*
3 tablespoons rolled oats	*Vegetable oil to mix*

Peel bananas. Cut in half lengthwise, then crosswise. Toss with lemon juice and spoon into oven-proof dish. In a small bowl mix rolled oats with flour, cinnamon, and just enough oil to mix. Sprinkle over bananas. Broil for 3 or 4 minutes about 6″ from heat.

Cool slightly before serving, since fruit is very hot. Serve warm and top with ice cream or sherbet. Serves 4.

• Variations

Broiled Apple Crisp, Broiled Blueberry Crisp, Broiled Peach Crisp, Broiled Pear Crisp. Substitute fruits and prepare as above.

FRUIT GRANOLA CRISP

One of our favorites—sweet fruit with a crunchy granola topping.

4 cups sliced fresh fruit
2 tablespoons melted butter
1 teaspoon lemon juice

1 tablespoon cinnamon
½ to 1 cup granola (mixed oats, nuts, seeds, and dried fruit)

Combine sliced fruit with butter, lemon juice, and cinnamon and mix. Spoon fruit into an oiled shallow baking dish and sprinkle liberally with granola. Bake at 325 degrees for 40 to 45 minutes or until fruit is tender.

Serve warm or chilled. Serves 6.

• Recommended Fruits

Apples, bananas, blueberries, peaches, pears, pineapple.

GRANDMA'S APPLESAUCE CAKE

Spicy apple cake served with warmed applesauce.

Cake:
¼ cup butter, softened
3 large eggs
½ cup apple juice
½ cup unsweetened applesauce
2 cups unbleached white flour
2 teaspoons baking powder
1 teaspoon baking soda

2 teaspoons cinnamon
½ cup raisins (optional)
1 fresh apple, washed, peeled, cored, and thinly sliced

Topping:
Unsweetened applesauce, warmed over medium heat

In a medium-sized bowl beat together until creamy butter, eggs, apple juice, and applesauce. Add flour, baking powder, baking soda, and cinnamon. Beat well. Stir in raisins if desired.

Oil and flour an 8″ square baking pan. Line the bottom of the pan, one layer deep, with thinly sliced apple. Spoon batter over apples and smooth top. Bake at 350 degrees for 25 to 30 minutes or until well-browned. Invert onto a wire rack to cool, apple side up.

Serve apple side up on individual dessert plates and spoon warm applesauce over each portion. Serves 6.

CRAZY FRUIT UPSIDE-DOWN CAKE

Soft, delicious cake with juicy fruit topping.

Topping:

2 or 3 cups chopped fruit (see recommendations below)

1 tablespoon vegetable oil

½ to 1 teaspoon cinnamon or nutmeg

2 tablespoons milk

½ cup unsweetened fruit juice (apple, pineapple, or orange)

1½ cups unbleached white flour

½ teaspoon baking soda

1 teaspoon baking powder

Cake:

1 large egg

¼ cup vegetable oil

To prepare topping, toss together fruit, oil, and spice to taste. Spoon mixture into an oiled 8″ square casserole dish.

To prepare cake, beat together egg, oil, milk, and fruit juice. Add flour, baking soda, and baking powder. Beat well. Pour batter over fruit. Smooth evenly in casserole dish. Bake at 350 degrees for 30 minutes. Cool until just warm and turn out onto a serving dish.

Serve plain, or with ice cream or whipped cream. Serves 4 to 6.

• Recommended Fruit

Apples, whole blueberries, peaches, pears, pineapple, bananas.

FRUIT CASSEROLE CAKE

Very light, sweet casserole that melts in your mouth.

2 eggs, separated

1 tablespoon mashed banana (mash ripe banana with a fork)

¼ cup unsweetened fruit juice

¾ cup unbleached white flour

2 teaspoons baking powder

2 cups chopped fresh fruit (see recommendations below)

Beat egg whites until stiff and set aside. Beat together egg yolks, mashed banana, and fruit juice. Add flour and baking powder and mix. Add chopped fruit together with egg whites and mix gently by hand until blended. Spoon into lightly oiled 8″ square baking casserole. Bake at 350 degrees for 20 to 25 minutes or until firm to the touch and lightly browned.

Serve warm, plain or topped with whipped cream. Serves 6.

• Recommended Fresh Fruit

Bananas, whole blueberries, pears, peaches, pineapple.

FRUIT SOFT CAKE

A fruit-filled hot casserole cake.

Cake:

⅔ cup mashed banana (mash ripe banana with a fork)

2 large eggs

1 cup unbleached white flour

2 teaspoons baking powder

½ cup chopped nuts

2 or 3 cups chopped fruit

Nutmeg or cinnamon (optional)

Topping:

Fruit Pudding (see pages 91–96)

Beat together mashed banana and eggs until creamy. Add flour and baking powder and beat well. Stir in chopped nuts and fruit. Pour mixture into an oiled and floured 8″ square baking pan. Bake at 350 degrees for 20 to 25 minutes or until browned.

Spoon onto dessert plates and top with fruit pudding. Garnish with chopped fresh fruit if desired. Serves 4.

• *Recommended Fruit*

Apples, whole blueberries, peaches, pears, pineapple, bananas.

Fruit Sauces
and Puddings

Fruit Sauces

Fruit sauces are so simple to make and yet add such elegance, color, and a delicious aroma to desserts. Just about any fruit can be blended into a rich vitamin-filled sauce. Fresh raspberries and blackberries are delectable floating in a creamy pineapple sauce. Or drizzle strawberry sauce over Banana Ice Cream (pages 111–112) and sprinkle with nuts for an all-time favorite. Fruit sauces enliven fresh and baked fruit, pies, pancakes, and fruit-sweetened ice cream and sherbet.

Helpful Hints

1. For the most flavorful sauces, choose good-quality ripe fruit.
2. Always wash fruit thoroughly, remove the skin, and core or pit before blending. Whip chopped fruit in a food processor or blender until smooth.
3. Flavor sauces with a sprinkle of spice or juice. Nutmeg, cinna-

mon, cloves, and ginger add a special zing to sauces. Apple, pineapple, banana, and pear all perk up with a dash of spice. Lemon and lime juices are especially effective in exotic sauces such as papaya, guava, and mango.

4. Fruit sauces are at their peak of essence and flavor when they are created, so use them as soon after blending as possible. Refrigerate sauces to retain quality.

Some Fruits Suitable For Sauces

apple	mango	plum
banana	papaya	raspberry
blueberry	peach	strawberry
cherry	pear	
guava	pineapple	

APPLE SAUCE

Whip up easily from fresh apples. No cooking.
6 medium apples, washed, peeled, cored, and sliced
Whip fruit in a food processor or blender until smooth. Yields 2 cups.

BANANA SAUCE

Creamy and very sweet.
1 cup mashed banana (mash ripe banana with a fork)
Whip mashed fruit in a food processor or blender until smooth. Yields ⅞ cup.

BLUEBERRY SAUCE

Tart blueberry flavor.
1 cup fresh blueberries, washed (remove stem pieces and discard damaged fruit)

Whip berries in a food processor or blender until smooth. Yields ⅔ cup.

CHERRY SAUCE

A sweet, dark-red sauce.
1 cup sliced sweet cherries, washed and pitted
Whip fruit in a food processor or blender until smooth. Yields ¾ cup.

MANGO SAUCE

Thick and rich sweet-tart flavor.
1 large, ripe mango, peeled and pitted
Whip fruit pulp in a food processor or blender until smooth. Yields ¾ cup.

PAPAYA SAUCE

A thick and creamy sauce with distinctive papaya flavor.
1 medium-sized ripe papaya, peeled and seeded
Whip fruit in a food processor or blender until smooth. Yields 1 cup.

PEACH SAUCE

A light and sweet orange sauce.
4 medium-sized fresh peaches, peeled, pitted, and sliced *1 16-oz. can sliced peaches in unsweetened juice, well drained*
or
Whip fruit in a food processor or blender until smooth. Yields 1¼ cups.

PEAR SAUCE

A light-brown sweet sauce.

3 medium-sized fresh pears, peeled, cored, and sliced

or

1 16-oz. can of sliced pears in unsweetened juice, well drained

Whip fruit in a food processor or blender until smooth. Yields 1 cup.

PINEAPPLE SAUCE

A thick and very sweet sauce.

1 20-oz. can crushed pineapple in unsweetened juice

Whip contents of can (including juice) in a food processor or blender until smooth. Yields 2¼ cups.

PLUM SAUCE

A blue-purple sauce that is full of rich plum flavor.

6 to 8 medium-sized plums, peeled and pitted

Whip fruit pulp in a food processor or blender until smooth. Yields 1 cup.

STRAWBERRY SAUCE

A brilliant red sauce with sweet strawberry flavor.

1 pint fresh strawberries, washed (remove stems and discard damaged fruit)

Whip berries in a food processor or blender until smooth. Yields 1⅛ cups.

Fruit Puddings

Fruit puddings stand alone as a light, delicious dessert and make an excellent filling for cream pies and puff pastry. Any fruit sauce can be transformed into a rich and thick pudding. Simply combine blended fruit with recommended thickening agent, simmer over low heat until the mixture has set, and chill. These fruit puddings can be garnished with sliced fresh fruit, shredded coconut, or just about any other topping. Spoon into dessert goblets and add cream, yogurt, fruit, nuts, prepared toppings (see index), or spices for a festive, easy-to-prepare, healthful treat.

Helpful Hints

1. For the most flavorful puddings choose good-quality, ripe fruit. Blend chopped fresh or well-drained canned fruit in a food processor or blender until smooth. This produces a fruit sauce.
2. Mix together fruit sauce and thickening agent in a blender or food processor to produce a smooth pudding.
3. If possible, cook puddings in a large double boiler over boiling water to insure even, slow, gentle cooking. If using a saucepan, stir constantly and quickly for creamy, even smoothness.
4. It is essential to stir often as pudding thickens. Using a large wooden spoon or wire whisk, stir and beat, scraping the bottom and sides well.
5. Cook puddings long enough so that they reach a decidedly thick consistency. Usually this requires cooking at least several minutes after the pudding reaches a boil.
6. When partially cooled, pudding may be spooned into sherbet dishes, goblets, or pastries. If pudding is completely cooled before you use it in a recipe, whip it well with a wooden spoon for a satiny smooth texture.
7. Always keep puddings refrigerated.

Thickening Agents

Arrowroot—This is a fine white powder made from the root of the arrowroot plant. It is an excellent thickening agent, mixes well with fruits, and has no noticeable flavor of its own. Simply combine well with fruit sauce, heat, and stir constantly as mixture thickens. For thickening, substitute half as much arrowroot as the required amount of flour.

Cornstarch—This is a fine white powder made from the endosperm portion of corn kernels. It is primarily used as a thickening agent. Combine well with fruit sauce, bring to a boil, and stirring constantly, continue to cook just a minute or two more. Remove from the heat and cool. As with arrowroot, substitute half as much cornstarch as the required amount of flour.

Flour—It is convenient and easy to use as a thickening agent. The primary disadvantage is that it may add a flavor of its own when used in substantial amounts. Blend in with fruit sauce, bring to a boil, and cook until thickened. Stir and whip constantly as mixture thickens for best results.

• Note

2 tablespoons flour = 1 tablespoon arrowroot or cornstarch. If mixture fails to thicken sufficiently, simply combine additional thickening agent with cold water (approximately 1 tablespoon thickener to 2 tablespoons water) and mix until smooth. Gradually stir into warm pudding mixture. Heat and continue stirring until sufficiently thickened.

Recommended Fruits for Pudding

apple	mango	pineapple
banana	papaya	plum
blueberry	peach	strawberry
guava	pear	sweet cherry

APPLE PARFAIT PUDDING

A chunky pudding filled with apple bits and served with nuts.

Pudding:
6 cups chopped apple (about 9 apples, peeled and cored)
¼ cup cornstarch

Lemon juice
Cinnamon and nutmeg to taste

Topping:
1 cup chopped walnuts

Put half of the chopped apples in a blender and blend with cornstarch. Combine with lemon juice and spices to taste. Pour into the top of a double boiler and cook over medium heat, stirring, as mixture reaches a boil and thickens. Add remaining chopped fruit and cook just until tender. Cool.

Layer apple pudding and chopped nuts in tall dessert goblets, ending with nuts. Chill and serve. Top with whipped cream if desired. Serves 6.

SOUTHERN PEACH PUDDING

An easy but elegant fruit-filled pudding topped with cream and grated pecans.

Pudding:

6 cups chopped peaches (about 10 peaches, peeled and pitted)

¼ cup cornstarch

Cinnamon or nutmeg (optional)

Topping:

½ pint heavy cream

1 cup grated pecans

Put half of the chopped peaches in a blender or food processor and blend with cornstarch until smooth. (Add cinnamon or nutmeg to taste if desired). Pour into the top of a double boiler, bring to a boil over medium setting, and stir constantly. Mixture will thicken. Add remaining chopped peaches and cook just until tender. Spoon into individual sherbet dishes and chill. Shortly before serving, whip heavy cream and spoon over pudding. Top with grated pecans and serve immediately. Serves 6.

FRESH PEAR PUDDING

Bits of pear in a smooth, light pudding.

Pudding:

4½ cups blended pear (whip chopped fresh or canned pear in a blender or food processor)

⅜ cup cornstarch

½ teaspoon nutmeg

Topping:

1 cup Banana Ice Cream (see pages 111–112)

1 cup chopped walnuts

Combine blended pear and cornstarch in a blender. Add nutmeg and blend well. Heat in a double boiler over medium setting, stirring constantly as mixture reaches a boil and thickens. Remove from heat, cool, and spoon into individual serving dishes.

To serve, top each with a spoonful of banana ice cream and a scoop of chopped nuts. Serves 6.

PINEAPPLE COCONUT NUT PUDDING

A crunchy pudding filled with fruit, nuts, and coconut.

2 20-oz. cans unsweetened crushed   ¼ cup chopped walnuts
   pineapple   1 teaspoon nutmeg
3 tablespoons cornstarch   ¼ teaspoon cinnamon
¼ cup flaked coconut

Drain the crushed pineapple through a strainer, saving the juice in a bowl. Reserving two cups of pineapple pieces, put the rest in a blender. Add all the juice and the cornstarch. Blend well. Pour into the top of a double boiler and, stirring constantly, thicken over medium heat. Mixture will reach the consistency of paste. Add coconut, nuts, spices, and the reserved pineapple pieces. Stir, remove from heat, cool, and refrigerate. Serves 6.

SIMPLE PLUM PUDDING

A quick, easy, slightly tart pudding.

4½ cups blended plum (whip plum pulp in a food processor or blender until
   smooth) and ⅜ cup cornstarch

Combine blended plum and cornstarch in a blender and mix well. Pour mixture into the top of a double boiler. Heat over medium setting, stirring constantly, as mixture reaches a boil and thickens. Remove from heat and refrigerate.

Serve in dessert bowls topped with whipped cream. Serves 6.

PINEAPPLE PUDDING

Tangy pudding topped with orange-flavored whipped cream.

Pudding:

4½ cups blended pineapple (whip chopped pineapple in a blender/-processor)

⅓ cup cornstarch

Topping:

½ pint heavy cream

½ teaspoon orange extract

½ cup flaked coconut

Whip blended pineapple and cornstarch in a blender. Pour into the top of a double boiler. Heat over medium setting, stirring constantly as mixture reaches a boil and thickens. Remove from heat and chill.

To serve, spoon into individual sherbet dishes. Beat heavy cream and orange extract at high speed until fluffy, spoon onto pudding portions, and sprinkle each with flaked coconut. Serves 6.

Crackers, Jams, and Spreads

Crackers

Crisp, light, and crunchy, crackers are a great snack. Fruit-sweetened crackers, compact wafers of flour, nuts, and fresh fruit, are unusually flavorful. Cheese and crackers will never be the same again once you have enjoyed crackers with the tang of orange or pineapple. Topped with cheese, served alone or with a dip, fruit-sweetened crackers are an unusual and delicious treat for guests. Spread them with peanut butter and jam for a room full of hungry kids, with cream cheese for a delicious late-night snack. There is no limit to the variety of crackers you can create using flour, nuts, seeds, herbs, and nature's delicious fruit flavors.

Helpful Hints

1. Always bake in a preheated oven.
2. Oil baking sheets unless otherwise noted.
3. Prick with a fork before baking for flat crackers.

4. Check several times during baking, as the thinness of the crackers will influence baking time.
5. Cool completely before storing in covered containers.
6. Crackers freeze well; wrap securely.
7. To crisp frozen crackers, thaw and bake at 325 degrees for 5 minutes.

Recipe Suggestions

Flour Substitutions—Refer to Fortify with Flour (see pages 140–142) for recommended flours, substitution guidelines, and suggested amounts.

Cracker Mix-In—Any of the following may be mixed into cracker dough to increase nutritional value and add texture and taste: wheat germ, jam, corn meal, ground rolled oats, grated cheese, flaked coconut, cinnamon, ground nuts, powdered milk, nutmeg, nut butter, poppy seeds, finely grated carrot, mashed fruit, or seed butter.

Cracker Bake-On—Before baking, sprinkle crackers with any of the following and press into crackers: poppy seeds, garlic powder, nutmeg, ground nuts, sesame seeds, oregano, onion powder, corn meal, caraway seeds, cinnamon, grated cheese, or wheat germ.

Cracker Toppings—Frost cooled crackers with any of the following. Either frost each individual cracker or coat half and cover with remaining frosting. Suggestions include jam, nut butter, cream cheese, cottage cheese, seed butter, or your choice of one of the Spread-On Toppings (see page 129).

BANANA SESAME CRACKERS

Delicious combination of banana and crunchy sesame seeds.

½ cup mashed banana (mash ripe banana with a fork)
¼ cup vegetable oil
3 tablespoons water
1½ cups sesame seeds
2 cups unbleached white flour (approximately)

In a medium-sized mixing bowl beat together mashed banana, oil, and water until blended. Stir in sesame seeds. Gradually add flour, using just enough to form a moist, slightly sticky dough. Knead a few minutes on a floured surface. Roll dough into small balls the size of grapes and press between palms to form flat crackers. Prick with a fork. Bake on oiled baking sheets at 350 degrees for 15 minutes or until lightly browned. Cool. Yields 2 to 3 dozen.

PEANUT BUTTER CRACKERS

A crisp cracker to spread with jam.

1 cup unbleached white flour   *2 tablespoons peanut butter*
2 tablespoons vegetable oil   *¼ to ⅓ cup milk*

Combine flour, oil, and peanut butter in a bowl. Gradually add milk, using just enough to form a soft dough. Knead several minutes and roll out on a lightly floured surface to ⅛" thickness. Cut into desired shapes with cookie cutters and place on oiled baking sheets. Prick with a fork. Bake at 325 degrees for 12 minutes or until lightly browned. Cool on wire racks. Yields 4 dozen.

SESAME FRUIT CRACKERS

Delicious, light, and flaky. Fragile, so handle carefully.

2 cups unbleached white flour   *1 cup sesame seeds*
⅓ cup vegetable oil   *½ teaspoon salt (optional)*
¼ cup unsweetened fruit juice (ap-
proximately)

In a mixing bowl combine flour and oil. Add fruit juice gradually, using just enough to form a soft, pliable dough. Add sesame seeds and salt. Mix well by hand. Separate into two pieces and roll each out on a floured surface to ⅛" thickness, cut into desired shapes, place on oiled baking sheets, and prick with a fork. Bake at 325 degrees for 20 to 25 minutes or until browned around the edges. Cool. Yields 5 dozen.

• Recommended Fruit Juices

Apple, grapefruit, orange, pineapple, papaya.

DAIRY CRACKERS

Mildly tart. Spread with peanut butter or jam.

1 cup unbleached white flour   *⅓ cup yogurt (approximately)*
2 tablespoons vegetable oil

Mix together flour and oil. Gradually add yogurt, using just enough to form a soft dough. Knead and roll out on floured surface to ⅛" thickness, cut with cookie cutters, place on oiled baking pans, and prick with a fork. Bake at 325 degrees for 10 minutes or until lightly browned. Cool on wire racks. Yields 3 dozen.

SOFT PRETZELS

Easy and delicious. Let the kids help, too!

4 cups unbleached white flour   *unsweetened fruit juice*
2 tablespoons vegetable oil   *1 egg*
2 tablespoons granular yeast   *Salt (optional)*
1½ cups lukewarm,

Combine two cups flour, oil, yeast, and fruit juice in a large mixing bowl; beat with an electric mixer a few minutes. Add remaining flour and knead for 10 minutes or until smooth and elastic. Add more flour if sticky. Pinch off pieces of dough and form into long snakes. Twist into desired shapes and place on oiled baking sheets. Leave in warm place half an hour to rise. Brush with beaten egg and sprinkle with salt. Bake at 450 degrees for 15 minutes or until browned. Cool. Yields 30 or more.

SUNFLOWER CRACKERS

Rich sunflower flavor with a trace of salt.

1 cup unbleached white flour   *2 tablespoons vegetable oil*
3 tablespoons sunflower seed butter   *3 tablespoons water*
(blend seeds in a food processor)   *⅛ to ¼ teaspoon salt (optional)*

Combine flour, sunflower seed butter, and oil. Gradually add water, using just enough to form a soft dough. Add salt if desired.

Knead and roll out on floured surface to ⅛" thickness. Cut into shapes, place on oiled baking sheets, and prick with a fork. Bake at 325 degrees for 10 minutes or until browned. Cool. Yields 3 or 4 dozen.

SWEET CRACKERS

Fruit juice flavor in a crispy cracker. A delightful flavor surprise.

2 cups unbleached white flour
1 cup unsweetened fruit juice
⅓ cup vegetable oil

2 cups unbleached white flour (approximately)
Salt (optional)

In a bowl mix together two cups of flour, fruit juice, and oil until smooth. Add remaining flour, using just enough to form a soft dough. Season dough with salt if desired. Roll out half at a time on a lightly floured surface to ⅛" thickness. Cut with cookie cutters and place on oiled baking sheets. Prick with a fork. Bake at 375 degrees for 10 minutes or until lightly browned around the edges. Cool. Yields 4 or 5 dozen.

• Recommended Fruit Juices

Apple, grapefruit, orange, pear, pineapple, papaya, and mixed fruit juices.

NICE 'N FRUITY CRACKERS

Blended fruit give these crackers a lively taste.

1 cup unbleached white flour
2 tablespoons oil

⅓ cup blended fruit (whip chopped fresh or canned fruit in a blender until smooth)

In a medium-sized mixing bowl mix together flour and oil until crumbly. Gradually add blended fruit, using just enough to form a soft dough. Knead and roll out on a floured surface to ⅛" thickness. Cut with a cookie cutter and place on oiled baking sheets. Prick with a fork. Bake at 325 degrees for 15 minutes or until lightly browned. Cool on wire racks. Yields four dozen or more.

TAHINI CRACKERS

Hearty sesame flavor. Delicious spread with peanut butter.

1 cup unbleached white flour   *2 tablespoons vegetable oil*
2 tablespoons tahini (available in   *¼ teaspoon salt (optional)*
health food stores, or grind ses-   *3 tablespoons water*
ame seeds in a food processor
until creamy)

Combine flour, tahini, oil, and salt and blend well. Gradually add water, using just enough to form a soft dough. Roll out dough on floured surface to ⅛" thickness, cut into shapes, place on oiled baking sheets, and prick with a fork. Bake at 325 degrees for 10 minutes or until lightly browned. Cool on wire racks. May be spread with cream cheese or jam. Yields 3 or 4 dozen.

Jams, Fruit Butters, and Spreads

Fruit jams are so easy to make and so full of naturally concentrated fruit sweetness that once you have tasted homemade, you will never again settle for sugar-sweetened jelly. Ripe and juicy fruits, blended to a sauce and heated over low temperature, yield rich, condensed jams and spreads. Fruits can be combined into an endless variety of delectable jams, satiny smooth or dotted with ripe and juicy chunks of fresh fruit. Speckled, plump, golden bananas cook into a rich, sweet, fragrant sauce; crisp, fresh apples melt into a thick, brown, hearty jam; delicate peaches, pears, and strawberries soften into spreads that are fragrant and light. The rich aroma of fresh fruit, slowly heating on the stove, releasing its delicious perfumes, will fill your kitchen.

Helpful Hints

1. For the most flavorful jams choose good-quality, ripe fruit.
2. Always wash fruit thoroughly, remove the skin, and core before blending.

3. If the sauce is fairly thin, such as strawberry or blueberry, combine it with equal amounts of a thick sauce like pineapple, banana, or papaya to decrease cooking time and increase the volume of jam. You will also discover delicious new flavors.

4. Don't be timid about blending fruits. Banana blends well with most sauces. Try apple and peach, pineapple and papaya, and guava and strawberry. Create your own favorite combinations and serve them often.

5. Flavor jams with a sprinkle of spice or juice. Try nutmeg, cinnamon, clove, or ginger. Add a dash of lemon or lime juice to jams for slightly tart flavors. Just a bit should be added and absorbed into the jam as it cools.

6. For chunky jams, add fresh fruit slices or pieces to thickened fruit sauces during cooking and continue to simmer just until tender. Or add well-drained canned fruit pieces to warm jam. Apple, pear, and pineapple morsels blend well with many spreads. Use fruits that complement a jam (apple cubes in an apple jam) or fruits that contrast (crushed pineapple in a banana jam). Experiment with combinations and amounts, and you will discover unusual and tasty blends you will never find in any store.

7. As you will notice, the following recipes purposely yield a fairly small amount of jam. Because these jams are concentrated pure fruit, they are strikingly sweet and rich; therefore, a small amount goes a long way.

8. Always store jams and spreads refrigerated in covered containers. Best used within a week.

Some Fruits Suitable for Jams

apple	guava	pineapple
banana	mango	plum
blueberry	papaya	strawberry
date	peach	
fig	pear	

Recipe Suggestions

Jelly Substitute—Homemade jams readily replace jellies. Usually jams substitute splendidly right out of the refrigerator. If the spread is rather thick it may be blended with a complementary fruit juice or water in a food processor to the desired consistency. You will almost certainly prefer the robust fruit sweetness of your homemade jams to the sugary, syrupy sweetness of store-bought jellies.

Cookie Jams—As delicious as a fruit-sweetened cookie warm out of the oven is, nothing beats two cookies with sweet jam sandwiched in between. Try Lemon Moons (see page 17) with a pineapple spread for a zingy sweet and sour combination. Jams can also be spread on top of cookies or baked into them.

Jam Wafers—Crackers and jam are a long time favorite, but have you ever tried crackers, fresh from the oven, glazed with thick, sweet, homemade jam? The fruit melts into the warm, crisp crackers, adding a rich fruit flavor and a dash of color. Banana Sesame Crackers (pages 98–99) with a banana jam, Dairy Crackers (page 100) with a plum butter, and Peanut Butter Crackers (page 99) with a pineapple spread are a few of the many possible mouth-watering combinations.

Double Decker Dessert Bars—Spread generously between dessert bars, jams enhance flavor and appeal without interfering with the finger-food quality of this dessert, great for lunch boxes and traveling. These bars are a handy, no-nonsense snack.

Jammy Flapjacks—Spread your favorite jam over a warm pancake, top with a second, spread with more jam, top with a scoop of sherbet, and sprinkle liberally with chopped nuts for an unusual and festive dessert.

Jam Strip Pie—Coat the bottom of a prebaked pie shell liberally with jam. Pour pie filling over jam and refrigerate until set. To bake jam into a pie, simply spread jam on unbaked pie shell, gently add filling, and bake as directed. Fresh fruit pies blend well with jams. When the pie is cut, a delicious strip of jam flavor and color covers the bottom crust.

OLD-FASHIONED APPLE BUTTER

A rich brown jam with hearty apple flavor.

1 cup applesauce   Dash of cinnamon

In a small saucepan heat ingredients to a boil; turn to low and simmer, stirring occasionally, until mixture reaches desired thickness. Yields ½ cup.

AVOCADO BANANA SPREAD

A sweet jam with mild avocado flavor.

½ cup mashed ripe banana (mash   ½ cup mashed ripe avocado (mash
  with a fork)   with a fork)
                                   1 tablespoon lemon juice

Blend ingredients in a food processor or blender. Heat to a boil in a saucepan; turn to low and simmer, stirring occasionally, until mixture reaches desired thickness. Yields ½ cup.

SWEET BANANA JAM

A very concentrated jam.

2 cups ripe mashed banana (mash   2 tablespoons lemon juice
  banana with a fork)

Blend ingredients together until smooth. Heat to a boil in a saucepan; turn to low and simmer, stirring occasionally, until mixture thickens. Yields ⅓ cup.

TART BLUEBERRY BUTTER

A rich dark jam, slightly tart.

1 cup blended blueberries (whip berries in a food processor or blender until
  smooth)

Heat blended blueberries to a boil in a saucepan; turn heat to low and simmer, stirring occasionally, until mixture reaches desired thickness. Yields ⅓ cup.

DATE SPREAD

Very sweet and rich.

8 medium-sized dates, pitted   *Water or unsweetened fruit juice*

Blend dates in a food processor or blender until thick and pasty. Gradually add water or fruit juice, using just enough to dilute mixture to desired consistency. Yields ¼ cup.

FIG SPREAD

Dark brown jam with fresh fig flavor.

4 whole dried figs   *Water or unsweetened fruit juice*

Remove stems and blend figs in a food processor or blender until smooth. Gradually add water or fruit juice to reach desired consistency. Yields ¼ cup.

MANGO JAM

Slightly tart and delicious.

1 cup blended mango (whip chopped fruit in a food processor or blender until smooth)

Heat blended mango to a boil in a saucepan; turn to low and simmer, stirring occasionally, until mixture reaches desired thickness. Yields ⅓ cup.

CINNAMON PAPAYA JAM

Lightly sweet and spicy with cinnamon.

1 cup blended papaya (whip chopped fruit in a food processor or blender until smooth)   *Dash of cinnamon*

Heat ingredients to a boil in a saucepan; turn to low and simmer, stirring occasionally, until mixture reaches desired consistency. Yields ½ cup.

PEACH BUTTER

A sweet and tasty jam.
1 cup blended peach (whip chopped fruit in a food processor or blender until smooth)
Heat blended peach to a boil in a saucepan; turn to low and simmer, stirring occasionally, until mixture reaches desired thickness. Yields ¼ cup.

PEAR JAM

A lightly sweet brown jam.
1 cup blended pear (whip chopped fruit in a food processor or blender until smooth)   *1 teaspoon lemon juice*
Heat ingredients to a boil in a saucepan; turn to low and simmer, stirring occasionally, until mixture reaches desired thickness. Yields ½ cup.

SPICY PINEAPPLE SPREAD

A very rich, deep yellow spread.
1 cup blended pineapple (whip fruit in a food processor or blender until smooth)   *¼ teaspoon cinnamon*
Heat ingredients to a boil in a saucepan; turn to low and simmer, stirring occasionally, until mixture reaches desired thickness. Yields ⅓ cup.

DARK PLUM BUTTER

Distinctive plum flavor.
1 cup blended plum (whip fruit in a food processor or blender until smooth)
   Heat fruit to a boil in a saucepan; turn to low and simmer, stirring occasionally, as mixture reaches desired consistency. Yields ¼ cup.

SWEET STRAWBERRY JAM

A rich pink jam.
1 cup blended strawberries (whip fruit in a food processor or blender until smooth)
1 cup mashed ripe banana (mash with a fork)

   Blend ingredients in a food processor or blender until smooth. Heat to a boil in a saucepan; turn to low and simmer, stirring occasionally, until mixture reaches desired thickness. Yields ½ cup.

Frosty Fruits, Ices, Ice Cream, and Sherbet

Frozen desserts conjure up visions of ice cream and popsicles, but there is no need to stop here. Freeze watermelon wedges, cantaloupe rings, and banana halves for quick and simple desserts. Keep a container of homemade sherbet tucked away for unexpected company or a last minute treat. And nothing beats a frozen sherbet pie for an impressive summer dessert. Whip up easy banana ice cream or fruit-sweetened popsicles and watch your kids enjoy healthy desserts full of vitamins and minerals.

Helpful Hints

1. Keep desserts frozen until ready to use.
2. Store securely sealed in plastic containers.
3. Dessert dishes and plates may be chilled before serving frozen desserts.

Recipe Suggestions

Frosty Mix-In—Shortly before serving, mix any of the following (chilled if possible) into sherbet or ice cream: raisins, carob chips, grated carrot, whole berries, ground nuts, toasted rolled oats, flaked coconut, chopped dates, granola, spices, chopped fresh fruit, or fruit extract.

Frosty Sprinkle-On—Any of the following may be sprinkled on frozen desserts as toppings: spices, grated carrot, flaked coconut, chopped dried fruit, carob chips, wheat germ, nuts, seeds, sliced fresh fruit, or a Sprinkle-On Topping (see pages 127–128).

Frosty Spoon-On Toppings—Spoon any of the following over frozen desserts and serve immediately: fruit sauce, fruit pudding, chopped fresh fruit, or any Spoon-On Topping (see pages 129–130).

Frosty Garnish—Enhance desserts by scooping various flavors of sherbet and ice cream on or next to any of the following: pancakes, dessert bars, pie, fruit bread, cake, pudding, fruit casserole, fresh fruit, muffins, sweet pastry, or fruit cocktail.

Sherbet Cup—Cut a fresh orange in half and scoop out the pulp to leave intact two orange rinds. Fill each with sherbet and freeze. Serve smothered with sliced banana and orange segments. Serves 2.

Juicy Sherbet Slush—In individual dessert bowls, pour chilled fruit juice over a scoop of sherbet. Garnish with chopped fresh fruit and a sprig of mint. Serve immediately.

Frozen Banana Cream Puffs—Prepare small cream puffs as directed (see page 55). Cut off the tops and fill each with thick Banana Ice Cream (see pages 111–112). Wrap in aluminum foil and freeze. Thaw slightly before serving. This is a delicious and elegant dessert that can be prepared in advance.

Frozen Sherbet Cream Puffs—Prepare as directed above; however, fill with sherbet. It is not necessary to thaw slightly before serving. Recommended sherbets include Apple Sherbet, Pineapple Sherbet, and Orange Sherbet. (See page 115.)

Sherbet/Ice Cream Sauce—In dessert goblets, drizzle cold fruit sauce over ice cream or sherbet. Sprinkle with wheat germ or flaked coconut and garnish with sliced banana and strawberries. Serve immediately.

Sherbet Soupy Sauce—In a chilled bowl gently mix together fruit sauce and sherbet, gradually adding just enough fruit sauce to reach desired thick, soupy consistency. Gently fold in fresh strawberries, blueberries, raspberries, and sliced banana. Spoon into chilled sherbet dishes and serve.

Ice Cream Float—Fill champagne glasses half full of fruit sauce, add a scoop of ice cream to each glass, garnish with a sprig of fresh mint, and serve.

AVOCADO BANANA ICE CREAM

Beautiful pale green color with sweet banana flavor. A family favorite.

¼ cup mashed avocado   *¼ cup plain yogurt*
2 medium-sized frozen bananas

Place mashed avocado in a food processor or blender and blend until smooth and creamy. Chop frozen bananas into ½" slices and add to avocado mixture. Process until smooth. Add yogurt and process just until mixed. Serve immediately. Delicious plain, or spoon onto a cantaloupe wedge, over fruit cocktail, cake, fruit bread, dessert bars, pie, or pudding. Serves 4.

BANANA ICE CREAM

This is always a hit with company. They can't believe banana is this sweet and creamy.

3 frozen bananas (allow ½ banana   Milk
*   per person)*

Peel and freeze ripe bananas. Just before serving, cut frozen bananas into ½" slices. Place in a food processor or blender and blend, adding just enough milk to reach a thick consistency. Do not add too much milk or you will make a milk shake. Serve immediately. Serves 6.

- Variations

Adding Banana Ice Cream to any plain food makes it a special dessert. Try putting it on a fruit cup, on a slice of fruit bread, a dessert bar, or a dish of canned fruit. Garnish ice cream with chopped nuts, wheat germ, coconut, or spices.

CREAMY FRUIT POPSICLES

Good nutrition and fun, too.

1 cup plain yogurt   ½ cup chopped fresh fruit

Combine ingredients in a blender and whip one minute. Pour into popsicle molds or paper cups with popsicle sticks inserted and freeze. Serves 3.

- Recommended Fruit

Apples, bananas, blueberries, peaches, pineapple, plums, pears.

FRUIT ICE CUBES

A delicious and colorful surprise in a cold beverage.

1 cup unsweetened fruit juice

Pour fruit juice in an ice cube tray and freeze until solid. Add to any fruit juice or beverage drink. Yields 14 ice cubes.

- Variations

Blend fresh or unsweetened canned fruit to a liquid and freeze in trays. Combine your own favorite fruit beverages and freeze mixtures. Mix colored ice cubes and flavors if desired.

WATERMELON WEDGES

Frosty cold, sweet watermelon pieces are popular all year long.

Watermelon (whole, half, or quarter)

Slice watermelon into thin slices and again into pie-shaped wedges. Lay flat on a baking sheet and freeze until firm. Cantaloupe wedges and honeydew wedges may be prepared the same way.

FROZEN JUICE POPSICLES

Easy to make and flavorful.
3 cups unsweetened fruit juice
   Pour fruit juice into popsicle molds or paper cups with popsicle sticks inserted and freeze until firm. Serves 6.
• Recommended Fruit Juices
Apple, pear, pineapple, orange, grapefruit, papaya.

FROZEN SAUCE POPSICLES

Thick, sweet popsicles rich in fruit flavor.
3½ cups chopped fresh or well-drained canned fruit in unsweetened juice
   Spoon fruit into a food processor or blender and whip until smooth. Pour into popsicle molds or paper cups with popsicle sticks inserted and freeze. Serves 6.
• Recommended Fruit
Apples, bananas, berries, mango, peaches, pears, pineapple.

FRUIT SLUSH

Cold, crunchy, and sweet. A real treat for kids.
1¼ cup chopped fruit (fresh,   8 to 10 ice cubes
   or canned in unsweetened juice)
   In a food processor or blender, blend fruit until smooth. Gradually add ice cubes until mixture reaches a thick slushy consistency. Serve immediately. Serves 3.
• Recommended Fruit
Apples, bananas, blueberries, peaches, pears, papaya, pineapple.

FROZEN BANANA POPSICLES

Creamy, sweet, and easy. A favorite with adults as well as kids.
2 ripe bananas   4 popsicle sticks

Peel bananas and cut each in half crosswise. Insert a popsicle stick into each cut end. Place on a baking sheet and freeze until firm. Serves 4.

• Variations

Before freezing, dip each banana into fruit juice and roll in flaked coconut or ground nuts. Freeze as directed. Or spread each with peanut butter and roll in wheat germ before freezing.

FROZEN CANTALOUPE RINGS

A fancy dessert for any occasion. Delicious!

1 whole ripe cantaloupe

Place cantaloupe on a cutting board and cut into thin slices as you would a loaf of bread. Remove the seeds and cut the rind from each ring. Lay rings flat on a baking sheet and freeze. Remove from freezer and allow to stand at room temperature 10 minutes before serving to thaw slightly. Place each slice on an individual dessert plate and fill the center with ice cream or sherbet, fruit pudding, chopped fresh fruit, sliced canned fruit, whipped cream, cottage cheese, or yogurt. Garnish with chopped nuts, flaked coconut, or toasted oat flakes. Serve immediately. Serves 6.

FRUIT SHERBET

Prepare in the afternoon and enjoy homemade sherbet for dinner.

2 cups of chopped fruit (fresh or canned)   *1 tray of ice cubes (12 to 14 cubes)*

Blend fruit in a blender. Gradually add ice cubes one at a time. Spoon mixture into an 8″ square pan and freeze until the mixture reaches sherbet consistency (about 1 to 1½ hours). Remove from freezer and serve. Serves 6.

• Recommended Fruit

Apples, pears, bananas, peaches, pineapple, papaya, mango.

FRUIT SNOW

Looks and tastes like fruit-flavored snow!

Prepare Fruit Sherbet as directed above, but allow to freeze until firm. Before serving break into pieces and whip in a food processor or blender until snow is formed. Serve immediately. Serves 6.

SHERBET—APPLE, ORANGE, PINEAPPLE

Sweet fruit juice and tart yogurt freeze to sherbet consistency. Won't freeze solid.

1⅓ cups unsweetened frozen con-
*   centrated fruit juice (apple, or-*
*   ange, or pineapple)*

two eggs, separated
2 cups plain yogurt

In a blender whip together concentrated fruit juice and two egg yolks until blended. Add yogurt and blend quickly, just enough to mix. Pour into an 8" square pan and freeze until center reaches slushy consistency and is almost frozen. Beat egg whites until stiff. Remove fruit mixture from freezer and blend with beaten egg whites just until mixed. Return to freezer in covered container and freeze. Serves 8.

FROZEN SHERBET PIE

You will have to taste this to believe how delicious a fruit-sweetened sherbet pie can be. A big hit for birthday parties or any other special occasion.

Pastry:
1 cup rolled oats
½ cup unbleached white flour
¾ cup flaked coconut
5 tablespoons vegetable oil
¼ teaspoon nutmeg
Unsweetened fruit juice

Filling:
1⅓ cups unsweetened frozen fruit
*   juice concentrate*
two eggs, separated
2 cups plain yogurt

Topping:
2 ripe bananas

To prepare pastry, combine ingredients except fruit juice and mix well. Gradually add fruit juice, using just enough to form a soft dough. Press into lightly oiled 9" pie pan and bake at 375 degrees for 15 minutes or until lightly browned. Cool and chill.

To prepare sherbet filling, whip concentrated fruit juice and egg yolks (reserve whites to use later) in a blender or food processor. Add yogurt and whip just until mixed. Pour into an 8" square pan and freeze until mixture reaches slushy consistency and is almost frozen. Beat egg whites until stiff. Remove partially frozen sherbet from freezer and blend with whipped egg whites on low blender speed just until mixed. Pour into prebaked pie crust and return to freezer. It will not freeze solid but will retain sherbet consistency.

When pie is frozen, top with sliced bananas and return to freezer. Allow pie to set 15 minutes at room temperature to soften slightly before serving. Serves 8.

• Recommended Frozen Fruit Juice Concentrates
Apple, orange, pineapple.

Fresh Fruit
and Dried Fruit

Fresh, fine-quality fruit offers a tremendous variety of distinctive flavors, aromas, textures and colors, and can be transformed into beautiful, nutritious, low-calorie desserts with very little preparation time. Here are some serving suggestions, or let the artist in you create original fruit combinations from nature's colorful and delicious palette.

Choosing Fresh Fruit

Always select good-quality fruit. Choose fruit that is free from bruises, cracks, or soft spots. If possible fruit should be ripe, but not overripe and soft. Apricots, avocados, bananas, cantaloupes, honeydew melons, peaches, and pears may be purchased underripe and allowed to ripen at room temperature or in the refrigerator. Blueberries, cherries, grapes, grapefruit, oranges, pineapple, plums, strawberries, and watermelon must be purchased ripe since they do not ripen once picked. Always refrigerate ripe fruit.

To avoid discoloration, toss cut fruit (apple, avocado, banana, peach, pear) with lemon or lime juice. Refrigerate and serve as soon as possible.

Helpful Hints to Prepare Fruit Cocktail

1. Always wash fruit well.
2. Chop, slice, or dice into portions small enough that they may easily be eaten with a teaspoon.
3. Treat fruits that discolor with lemon or lime juice, or add these fruits to the mixture just prior to serving.
4. Plan on ½ cup or more per serving.
5. Combine fruit and chill before serving to blend flavors.
6. Add fruit juice or fruit sauce if more liquid is needed.
7. Add a dash of lemon, lime, or cinnamon to perk up the flavor.
8. When making a fresh fruit cocktail, it is best to combine tart and sweet flavors and a variety of shapes, sizes, and colors.

Recommended Fruit Cocktail Combinations

- Grapefruit and orange sections, cinnamon stick.
- Pineapple spears, chopped mango, and lemon wedge.
- Watermelon, cantaloupe, and honeydew balls.
- Chopped pears, whole raspberries, and a slice of lime.
- Sliced apples, whole grapes, and crushed pineapple.
- Sliced peaches and pineapple juice, mint garnish.
- Whole blueberries and chopped kiwi fruit.
- Sliced bananas and strawberry halves.
- Honeydew balls, sliced papaya, and pomegranate seeds.
- Sliced apples, chopped apricots, sprig of mint garnish.
- Grape halves, avocado strips, and sliced cherries.
- Cubed pears, crushed pineapple, and sliced guava.

Suggestions for Serving Fruit Cocktail

Dessert Cups—Serve fruit cocktail in custard cups, sherbet dishes, hollowed-out fruit bowls (see below), champagne glasses, or parfait glasses.

Dessert Plates—Drain off liquid from fruit cocktail (reserve for a healthful beverage) and serve fruit on a bed of lettuce, flaked coconut, a pineapple or melon ring, or over any baked dessert or fruit pudding.

Fruit Cocktail Garnishes—Garnish fruit with a stick of cinnamon, sprinkle of nutmeg, slice of lemon, lime or kiwi fruit, sprig of fresh mint, bright cherry, raspberry or strawberry, a spray of pomegranate seeds, or a scoop of ice cream or sherbet. Also garnish with toppings or fruit puddings.

Fruit Sauce Cocktail—Mix together chopped or sliced fruit to fill a fruit bowl. Add nuts, flaked coconut, and dried fruit if desired. Drain off any liquid, reserving it for use in another recipe or as a refreshing beverage. Combine fruit mixture with your favorite fruit sauce, coating all ingredients with sauce, and adding a little extra. Spoon into individual sherbet dishes, garnish each with a wedge of lemon or lime, and serve.

Saucy Fruit Platter—Prepare a platter of sliced fresh fruit. Arrange in a pleasing pattern of varying colors, shapes, and sizes. Drizzle generously with fruit sauce and garnish with lemon wedges. Pass the platter to be served in individual dessert dishes.

Saucy Fruit Soup—Cut a fresh orange, grapefruit, or melon in half and hollow out the pulp to make bowls of fruit rind. Fill each bowl ½ full of fruit sauce and spoon in the reserved fruit pulp. Top each with whipped cream and garnish with fresh fruit.

Suggestions for Serving Fresh Fruit

APPLES

Apple–Cheese Star—Wash and core a fresh apple. In a small mixing bowl beat 3½ oz. of softened cream cheese with just enough milk to make it smooth and creamy. Spoon the mixture into the center of the apple and pack securely. Refrigerate until cheese is firm. With a sharp knife cut the apple & cheese into wedges, arranging wedges in a star pattern. Garnish the center with a sprig of mint and serve.

Cinnamon Apples—Toss chopped apples with lemon juice and cinnamon and spoon into individual serving dishes. Spoon chilled apple juice over all and serve immediately.

Apples and Cream—Gently mix chopped, fresh apple and a dash of cinnamon into whipped cream. Serve in individual dessert dishes and top with slivered almonds.

AVOCADOS

Avocado Filling—Mix together mashed avocado and cream cheese. Add a dash of lemon juice. Spread between crackers, cookies, or dessert bars and serve immediately.

Avocado Boat—Slice an avocado in half and carefully remove seed. Fill seed cavity with fruit pudding, ice cream, or sherbet. Serves two.

BLUEBERRIES

Heavenly Blueberries—Gently fold fresh blueberries into whipped cream. Spoon into individual dessert bowls and garnish with fresh sliced strawberries.

Berry Pineapple Dessert—Combine 1 can unsweetened crushed pineapple with an equal portion of fresh blueberries and chill.

Serve in sherbet dishes and top each with a scoop of Pineapple Sherbet (see page 115).

CANTALOUPE

Cantaloupe Fruit Bowls—Cut ripe melon in half and remove seeds. Scoop out pulp with a melon scooper or teaspoon, leaving a clean shell. Combine cantaloupe balls with honeydew balls, fresh strawberries, and your choice of chopped fruit. Spoon mixture into shells, add a spoonful of unsweetened frozen fruit juice concentrate to each, and garnish with a sprig of fresh mint.

Cantaloupe Rings—Slice a whole, ripe cantaloupe into 1" wide rings. Lay each ring on a cutting board and remove seeds and rind. On individual dessert dishes, fill each ring with chopped fresh fruit, sherbet, ice cream, fruit pudding, or cottage cheese.

CHERRIES

Cherry Spread—Combine finely diced cherries with softened cream cheese. Spoon into dates, celery stalks, or over crackers.

HONEYDEW MELON

Honeydew and Strawberries—Crush ripe, juicy strawberries and spoon over a chilled slice of melon.

Sour Melon—Drizzle fresh squeezed lime over honeydew slices.

ORANGES

Orange Cups—Wash orange and cut in half. Scoop out pulp, leaving rind intact. Fill each rind with chopped fruit or sherbet.

PEACHES

Peach Boats—Wash fresh peaches, cut in half lengthwise, and remove pit. Fill each cavity with ice cream, sherbet, chopped fresh fruit, yogurt, or fruit pudding.

Peaches and Coconut—Toss sliced peaches with flaked coconut and spoon into sherbet dishes.

PEARS

Spicy Pear—Wash, peel, core, and chop fresh pear. Toss with unsweetened pineapple juice and sprinkle with nutmeg. Serve chilled and topped with Banana Ice Cream (see pages 111–112).

Cottage Cheese and Pears—Wash, peel, core, and slice a fresh pear in half. Line serving dish with cottage cheese and top with pear halves, rounded sides up. Sprinkle with ground nuts or cinnamon.

PINEAPPLE

Pineapple Boats—On a cutting board, cut through fresh pineapple and leaf crown lengthwise. Carefully cut out the flesh using a small sharp knife to form two intact pineapple shells. Fill each shell with chopped pineapple pieces and other fresh fruit.

PLUMS

Plums and Berries—Combine peeled, chopped plums with whole or sliced strawberries and toss well. Crush a few strawberries for added juice, add, and chill. Serve in sherbet dishes.

Plum Banana Ice Cream—Cut plums into small pieces. Place on a cookie sheet and freeze. Combine with frozen banana pieces and prepare as for Banana Ice Cream (see pages 111–112).

STRAWBERRIES

Strawberries and Cream—Gently mix chilled, fresh strawberries with whipped cream. Spoon into individual dessert goblets and top each with a whole berry.

Strawberry Mix—Combine sliced, fresh strawberries, whole blueberries, and sliced banana. Toss with lime juice and serve in dessert bowls. Spoon fruit juice over fruits if desired.

WATERMELON

Watermelon Basket—Cut watermelon with a long, sharp knife as illustrated. First, 1″ from the center slice down vertically into melon, stopping halfway down. Next, starting at nearest end of melon, slice in half horizontally until cut meets vertical one. Carefully remove section. Repeat on the other side. With a melon scooper, scoop out the melon pulp, discarding the seeds. Mix melon balls with honeydew and cantaloupe balls, fresh berries, or your choice of fresh fruit. Spoon into watermelon basket and serve immediately or wrap and chill. Try cutting melon in a sawtooth pattern to form a fancy edge.

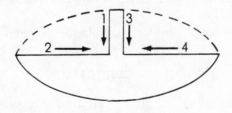

Dried Fruit

Dried fruit provides a concentrated form of nutrients, sweetness, vitamins, and minerals, and is excellent baked into fruit breads or stirred into ice cream. Add morsels of dried fruit to fruit puddings, pie fillings, cookie batter, coffee cake toppings, and fresh fruit compotes for a spark of flavor.

Helpful Hints

1. To plump up raisins, bring to a boil in a small saucepan of water, remove from heat, and let stand covered 10 minutes.
2. Cut dried fruit with scissors, or use a sharp knife on a cutting board. Occasionally dip cutting blade into cold water for easier cutting.

Cooking Dried Fruit

Soaking—Unpackaged dried fruit should be soaked in a small amount of water for ½ hour before cooking. Packaged dried fruit does not require soaking.

Pressure Cooking—Place dried fruit in a pressure cooker, adding approximately twice as much water as fruit. Process at 15 pounds of pressure for approximately 8 to 10 minutes, following instructions available in your pressure cooker information booklet.

Saucepan Cooking—Place dried fruit in a saucepan. Add half as much water as fruit and simmer, covered, over low heat 30 to 40 minutes or until soft. Some packaged dried fruits are processed to reduce cooking time; in this case follow package directions.

Storage—Store cooked fruit refrigerated in covered containers.

Recipe Suggestions

Dried Fruit Mix-In—Stir dried fruit into any of the following: jam, yogurt, fruit pudding, pie filling, fruit casserole, sherbet, nut butter, cream cheese, fresh fruit, frozen desserts, tart fillings, fruit sauce, ice cream, cottage cheese, or any dessert batter.

Dried Fruit Bake-On—Sprinkle dried fruit or nuts over any of the following and bake as directed: cake batter, fruit casserole, fruit bread batter, cookie batter, fruit pie, muffin batter, baked or broiled fruit, pancake batter, or dessert bar batter.

Dried Fruit Sprinkle-On—Sprinkle chopped dried fruit over any of the following and serve: ice cream, cottage cheese, pancakes, custard, sherbet, fruit pudding, fruit cocktail, yogurt, canned fruit, or pie.

STUFFED DRIED FRUIT

Stuff pitted dates or prunes with nut or seed butter, jam, nut meats, or cream cheese. Serve whole, or cut into strips and use as a garnish over fresh fruit, cottage cheese, yogurt, or pudding.

DRIED FRUIT BARS

Combine two cups chopped dried fruit and two cups chopped nuts. Mix well in a food processor, blender, or food chopper. Press into oiled 8" square pan and refrigerate until firm. With a sharp knife cut into bars.

DRIED FRUIT BALLS

Combine two cups chopped dried fruit and ¾ cup chopped nuts in a food processor, blender, or food chopper. Shape into 1" round balls, roll in coconut, and refrigerate.

DRIED FRUIT COMPOTE

Combine dried fruits to equal two cups. Wash and place in a medium-sized saucepan, adding just enough water to cover. Simmer, covered, for 15 minutes or until tender. Drain off excess water. Spoon into sherbet dishes and garnish with flaked coconut or fresh fruit. Serve warm.

FRUIT CANDY

A favorite with all ages.

Candy:

½ cup finely chopped dried fruit

½ cup sunflower seeds

½ teaspoon cinnamon

1 cup peanut butter

Topping:

⅓ cup flaked coconut

In a medium-sized mixing bowl mix together chopped dried fruit, sunflower seeds, and cinnamon. Gradually add peanut butter, using just enough to form a soft dough. Roll dough into 1″ balls and gently roll balls in flaked coconut. Place on cookie sheets and refrigerate until serving. Yields 2 or 3 dozen.

• Variations

Add wheat germ, chopped or ground nuts, sesame seeds.

• Recommended Dried Fruits

Apples, bananas, pears, dates, figs, pineapple, apricots.

Toppings

What easier way is there to turn a plain dessert into a fancy one? Plain canned pears bathed in pineapple sauce, sprinkled with cinnamon, and smothered with whipped cream become attractive and appetizing. Cakes, fruit breads, dessert bars, and muffins may be frosted with jams, nut butters, meringues, or creams and sprinkled with spices, nuts, coconut, and seeds. Cookies and pancakes, crackers, and fruit casseroles come to life with baked-in and spread-on toppings, which add nutritional value as well as visual appeal.

QUICK AND EASY SPRINKLE-ON TOPPINGS

To Prepare:	Toss together the following:	Yields:
Apple Spice Topping	2 large apples peeled, cored, and sliced; 1 T. lemon juice; cinnamon to taste	1½ cups
Crunchy Topping	½ cup roasted soybeans; 1 T. peanut butter; 2 T. ground sesame seeds	¾ cup

To Prepare:	Toss together the following:	Yields:
Granola Topping	1 cup of each of the following: rolled oats, chopped sunflower seeds, flaked coconut, chopped nuts; 1 T. vegetable oil; cinnamon to taste	4 cups
Pineapple Nut Topping	1 cup unsweetened crushed pineapple, well drained; ½ cup chopped nuts; nutmeg to taste	1½ cups
Date Nut Topping	¾ cup chopped dates; ¾ cup chopped nuts; ¾ cup flaked coconut; 1 T. unsweetened frozen fruit juice concentrate	2¼ cups
Nutty Pear Topping	1 t. lemon juice; 1½ cups chopped pear; 1 cup chopped nuts; 1 t. nutmeg	2½ cups
Pineapple Crunch Topping	1 cup unbleached white flour; 2 t. nutmeg; 2 cups chopped nuts; 4 to 5 T. vegetable oil; 1 cup unsweetened crushed pineapple, well drained	3 cups

Sprinkle toppings onto any of the following: cake, coffee cake, or fruit bread batters (bake as directed), fresh fruit cup, broiled or baked fruit (before or after cooking), pie, tarts, ice cream, sherbet, sliced fresh fruit, fruit pudding, custard, yogurt, cottage cheese, pie crusts, and cookies and muffins (before baking).

Mix toppings into any of the following: fruit cup, pie, tarts, meringue, pancakes, baked fruit casseroles, yogurt, fruit puddings, ice cream, sherbet, whipped cream, cottage cheese, and any batter (before baking).

QUICK AND EASY SPREAD-ON TOPPINGS

To Prepare:	Beat together the following:	Yields:
Cheese Fruit Sauce	1 8-oz. package cream cheese; ½ cup chopped fruit (blended in a blender until smooth)	1½ cups
Cranberry Cheese Nut Spread	1 8-oz. package cream cheese; approx. 2 T. milk (just enough for spreadable consistency); 1 cup chopped fresh cranberries; ½ cup ground walnuts	2 cups
Cheese Yogurt Topping	1 8-oz. package cream cheese; ⅓ cup yogurt; ½ cup finely chopped fruit	1½ cups
Creamy Fruit Sauce	1 cup cottage cheese; ½ to 1 cup blended fruit (whip chopped fruit in a blender until smooth)	1½ cups
Creamy Carob Frosting	½ cup mashed banana; 1 T. butter; 6 T. carob powder; 1 t. vanilla extract; 3 T. unbleached white flour	¾ cup

Spread toppings over any of the following: cakes, coffee cakes, dessert bars, crackers, cookies, pie crusts, pastries, muffins, or pancakes.

QUICK AND EASY SPOON-ON TOPPINGS

To Prepare:	Whip at high speed until peaks form:	Yields:
Whipped Cream	½ pint heavy cream	1¾ cups
Fruited Whipped Cream	½ pint heavy cream; ¼ cup blended fruit (whip chopped fruit in a blender until smooth)	1¾ cups

To Prepare:	Whip at high speed until peaks form:	Yields:
Carob Fluff Frosting	1 pint heavy cream; 1 t. vanilla extract; 6 T. carob powder	3 cups
Vanilla Topping	½ pint heavy cream; ½ t. vanilla extract	1¾ cups
Creamy Orange Topping	½ pint heavy cream; ½ t. orange extract	1¾ cups
Meringue Fluff	1 egg white; then fold in 2 T. blended fruit (whip chopped fruit in a blender until smooth); 1 cup chopped fruit, well drained; 1 cup chopped nuts	2 to 3 cups
Fruity Meringue Topping	1 egg white; 2 t. unsweetened frozen fruit juice concentrate	¾ cup
Yogurt Fluff	1 egg white; then stir in 1 cup yogurt	1½ cups
Zangy Fruit Topping	1 cup cottage cheese; 2 T. unsweetened frozen fruit juice concentrate	1 cup

MORE SPOON-ON TOPPINGS

To Prepare:	Mix and heat in a pan until thickened:	Yields:
Fruit Gel	1 cup unsweetened fruit juice; 1 T. cornstarch; ¼ t. lemon juice	⅞ cup
Fruit Spice Glaze	1 6-oz. can unsweetened frozen concentrated fruit juice; 1 6-oz. can water; ½ t. cinnamon; 1½ T. cornstarch	1 cup

To Prepare:	Mix and heat in a pan until thickened:	Yields:
Yogurt Sauce	1 cup yogurt; 1½ T. unsweetened fruit juice; 1½ T. cornstarch	1 cup

Spoon toppings over any of the following: sliced fresh fruit, pancakes, pie, melon halves, pineapple rings, custard, yogurt, fruit pudding, cake, cottage cheese, fruit cocktail, pastries, fruit bread, ice cream, sherbet, fruit casserole, beverages, tarts, muffins, and crêpes.

Fruit Beverages

Fruit juices are naturally sweet refreshments, rich in vitamins and minerals. Whipped in a blender, fresh ripe fruits dissolve into fragrant juices and nectars. Juices may be enjoyed alone or in endless mouth-watering combinations. Grapefruit juice has an agreeable tartness. Apple juice is clear and sweet, papaya juice rich and flavorful, pineapple juice strong and spicy, and orange juice isn't just for breakfast anymore. Health-minded individuals are increasingly choosing fruit juices for themselves and for their children and enjoying new combinations of these natural flavors more nutritious than anything the soda industry can offer. Serve elegantly and be inventive—the possibilities are endless.

Helpful Hints

1. Use frozen fruit juices promptly after defrosting.
2. Keep a variety of frozen fruit juice concentrates in your freezer. They will come in handy for adding a spoonful or two to perk up beverages. Hold a knife or spoon under hot running water

and use to dig or scoop out a spoonful or two of frozen concentrate. Cover the open can with foil or wrap in a plastic bag and replace in the freezer for future use.

3. Keep fruit juices refrigerated in covered containers to preserve vitamins and nutrients.

4. Use your own favorite fruit juice combinations in recipes that require juices.

Suggestions for Perking up Beverages

- Serve in chilled champagne glasses
- Add a squirt of lemon or lime
- Add a sprig of bright fresh mint
- Add a cherry, grape, or melon ball
- Perch a lemon, lime, or kiwi wedge on the rim of the glass
- Add ice cream or sherbet
- Sprinkle with flaked coconut
- Float fresh fruit in the beverage
- Add ice cubes made from colorful juices

Sherbet Punch—Place one pint of sherbet in a punch bowl and cover with one quart of chilled fruit juice. Stir gently and serve immediately for a delicious frosty party beverage.

QUICK AND EASY BEVERAGE COMBINATIONS

Fruit Sauces

1 cup applesauce   and 1 cup pear juice
1 cup banana sauce   and 1 cup pineapple juice
1 cup mango sauce   and 1 cup pear juice
1 cup peach sauce   and 1 cup apple juice
1 cup pear sauce   and 1 cup papaya juice
1 cup pineapple sauce   and 1 cup grapefruit juice
1 cup strawberry sauce   and 1 cup apple juice

- *Chill and serve*

Fruit Juices

1 cup apple juice	and 1 cup pineapple juice
1 cup grapefruit juice	and 1 cup mango juice
1 cup orange juice	and 1 cup grapefruit juice
1 cup papaya juice	and 1 cup guava juice
1 cup pear juice	and 1 cup papaya juice
1 cup pineapple juice	and 1 cup grapefruit juice

• *Mix in a blender with ice cubes and serve*

Fresh Fruit Beverages

1 cup chopped apple	and 1 cup grapefruit juice
1 cup chopped cantaloupe	and 1 cup apple juice
1 cup chopped guava	and 1 cup pear juice
1 cup chopped papaya	and 1 cup mango juice
1 cup chopped pear	and 1 cup pineapple juice
1 cup chopped watermelon	and 1 cup papaya juice

• *Combine in a blender and serve*

FRUIT BLEND

Easy, light, and delicious.

1 cup milk   *2 cups chopped fresh fruit*

Whip ingredients in a blender and serve immediately in a chilled glass. Serves 1.

• Recommended Fresh Fruits

Apples, apricots, bananas, blueberries, sweet cherries, peaches, pears, pineapples, plums, strawberries, papayas.

FRUIT FRAPPÉ

Sweet fruit flavor with pleasant yogurt tartness.

1 cup chopped fruit, fresh or canned   juice concentrate
in unsweetened juice   2 cups plain yogurt
1 6-oz. can unsweetened frozen fruit   2 eggs

Combine ingredients in a blender and whip until smooth. Serve chilled over ice, garnished with a dash of cinnamon or nutmeg, a pinch of toasted flaked coconut, a sprig of fresh mint, or a stick of cinnamon. Serves 4.

• Recommended Frozen Fruit Juice Concentrates
Apple, grapefruit, orange, pineapple.

JUICE SHAKE

Easy and delicious.

3 ounces (½ small can) unsweet-   2 cups milk
ened frozen concentrated fruit   Nutmeg or cinnamon
juice

In a blender, whip concentrated fruit juice and one cup milk until frothy. Add one cup more milk and blend quickly. Sprinkle with spices, and serve in chilled glasses, adding ice cubes made from colorful unsweetened fruit juices. Serves 3.

• Recommended Frozen Fruit Juice Concentrates
Apple, grapefruit, orange, pineapple.

CONCENTRATED FRUIT JUICE CRUNCH

A sweet, icy refreshment.

3 ounces (½ small can) unsweet-   7 to 9 ice cubes
ened frozen concentrated fruit   1 cup milk
juice

Whip together in a blender fruit juice concentrate and ice cubes, adding cubes gradually. Add milk and blend only a few seconds more. Pour into glasses and serve immediately. Serves 4.

• Recommended Frozen Fruit Juice Concentrates
Apple, grapefruit, orange, pineapple.

CREAMY SHAKE

Nutritious, thick, and sweet with fruit flavor.
½ cup plain yogurt
¾ cup chopped fresh fruit (any listed below)
 Blend ingredients in a blender until smooth. Serve immediately.
Serves 1.
• Variations
Apple Shake: Spicy sweet.
Banana Shake: Super thick, creamy.
Blueberry Shake: Delicious and—it's purple!
Mango Shake: Rich mango flavor.
Papaya Shake: Tropical island flavor.
Peach Shake: Lightly sweet and fragrant.
Pear Shake: Sweet and spicy.
Pineapple Shake: Very sweet.

APPENDIX I

BAKING WITH FRUIT—HELPFUL HINTS

Fruit Juices

Old favorites such as apple and orange juice are always tasty in desserts and can be perked up with a shake of nutmeg or cinnamon, a dash of lime, or a pinch of grated lemon. Experiment with combinations of juices and you will discover delicious new blends. Sweet juices combine especially well with tart ones; try pineapple and grapefruit, orange and lime, pear with a splash of lemon. For more exotic juices, such as papaya, mango, and guava, try your local health food store.

• Note
When substituting fruit juices for milk or water in traditional recipes that require baking, add ¼ to ½ teaspoon baking soda per cup of juice.

• Recommended Fruit Juices (available unsweetened)
Apple, apricot, guava, grapefruit, lemon, lime, mango, orange, papaya, peach, pear, pineapple.

Frozen Fruit Juice Concentrates

A highly concentrated natural sweetener, unsweetened fruit juice concentrate is easy to use and easy to store. Just a tablespoon or two added to batter gives a zing of flavor to cake, muffin, fruit bread, or cookie recipes, and can be used as the only sweetening agent or in combination with other fruit flavors. Store a variety of frozen fruit juice concentrates in your freezer within convenient reach for quick and easy use. A collection of 6-oz. cans fits neatly on the freezer door. Hold a knife or spoon under hot running water and use to dig or scoop out concentrate. After scooping out concentrate, simply cover

the open can with foil or wrap in a plastic bag and replace in the freezer for future use. Mix concentrates for unusual flavors. Substitute concentrates recommended in recipes to vary desserts. Replace part of the water or milk required in a recipe with a spoonful of exciting concentrated fruit flavor.
• Recommended Frozen Fruit Juice Concentrates (all unsweetened)
Apple, Grapefruit, Lemon, Lime, Orange, Pineapple

Fruit Sauces/Blended Fruit

Nothing surpasses fruit sauces for adding full rich flavor and body to baked goods. Delicate and light peach sauce, thick and luscious pineapple sauce, clear and spicy pear sauce, as well as countless others, are the basic foundation for many delectable recipes. Simply pour fresh or canned fruit into a blender and whip. For best results, use soon after preparing. Measure amounts accurately when adding fruit sauce to batters, and if the batter becomes so thick that it rides up the beaters, add a dash more sauce to thin it. This may occasionally happen because the thickness of blended fruit varies slightly depending upon the ripeness of the fruit and whether it is canned or fresh. Since fruit sauces are thicker than most liquids used in recipes, it is important to cook the dessert thoroughly to assure a completely baked product. It is for this reason that many recipes including a sizable proportion of fruit sauce suggest the dessert be baked until well browned. Cool before removing from the pan.
• Recommended Fruit Sauces
Apple, Banana, Berry, Cherry, Mango, Papaya, Peach, Pear, Pineapple, Plum, Strawberry

Fruit Morsels

Nothing is quite as delightful as biting into a muffin, warm from the oven, and discovering moist, sweet bits of fruit. Whether from a can, fresh, or dried, fruit morsels add sweetness, color, and texture to the simplest desserts. Most fruits can readily be chopped, sliced, or shredded into cakes, dessert bars, cookies, breads, muffins, and pancakes. Drain fruit pieces well before adding to recipes. Line the bottom of a pie shell with fruit, spoon pudding or additional fruit on top, and bake as directed. Stir fruit into pie fillings or arrange decoratively over fillings. Line oiled and floured cake pans with fruit slices, pour batter over, and bake. Toss fruit pieces in flour before adding to batter. This helps prevent fruit from sinking to the bottom during baking. Stir fruit into batter or arrange it over batter. Mix into cookie batter, bake into pancakes, sprinkle over muffins, and press into biscuits.

• Note

The only caution is to add fruit pieces conservatively to batters, since too many moist fruit pieces may cause the finished product to be undercooked.

• Recommended Fruit Morsels

Apple, Apricot, Banana, Blueberry, Cherry, Cranberry, Dates, Figs, Guava, Mango, Papaya, Peach, Pear, Pineapple, Raisins

APPENDIX II

FORTIFY WITH FLOUR

This book has been standardized with unbleached white flour for your convenience, since white flour is the most widely used baking flour. After you have made the healthful transition into fruit sweetening and are enjoying nature's natural flavors, I encourage you to go further and to enjoy nature's many fine whole grain flours. Many natural foods cookbooks are excellent sources of information and suggestions concerning the nutritional values and uses of the many available flours. Most of us are familiar with whole wheat, rice, rye, corn, and oat flour. Barley, buckwheat, potato, tapioca, peanut, sunflower, and soy flour are a bit more exotic but can be found in most health food stores.

Every flour is unique in its particular composition of nutrients, distinctive flavor, and often texture. Some are derived from grains, others from seeds or vegetables. It is for these reasons that each flour interacts differently with the other ingredients in a recipe and substitutions are a little tricky.

The following descriptions of flours suggest some guidelines for substitutions in recipes, but personal experience is the best teacher. Begin by substituting a small portion (¼ cup) per recipe to see what effects it will have on flavor, texture, rise, and consistency. You will probably discover that flours other than white tend to produce drier desserts. Try adding a little fruit sauce, mashed banana, milk, or butter to compensate for dryness. Some desserts, especially those containing thick fruit sauces or mashed banana, adapt well to partial or total substitutions. Fruit juice–sweetened recipes may be more sensitive to changes. By all means mix several flours for variety and nutritional values. Expect an occasional failure as you experiment with new combinations, and don't forget to make notations next to recipes regarding the flours used and the proportions you prefer for easy future reference.

Barley Flour—Contains a slight amount of gluten. It is a nutritious flour, gives a sweet, moist quality and a pleasant nutty flavor to baked goods. Substitute barley flour for a small portion of suggested flour.

Buckwheat Flour—The dark flour is made from ground buckwheat and the light from sifted buckwheat meal. Both are heavy, grainy, and solid, commonly used in buckwheat pancakes. Buckwheat flour is often substituted for a small portion of flour in baked goods. The amount varies according to taste and texture preferences.

Corn Flour—Made by finely grinding corn kernels or as a by-product in the production of corn meal. It has a pleasant corn flavor and may be substituted for corn meal or a portion of suggested flour in recipes. It also may be used as a thickener.

Corn Meal—Coarsely ground corn kernels. White corn meal is ground white corn. Yellow corn meal is ground yellow corn, and it is higher in vitamin A than white corn meal. Both have distinctive corn flavors and contribute a crumbly texture to baked goods. Substitute for small amounts of suggested flour in moist desserts and sprinkle over casseroles and batters before baking.

Oat Flour—Produced from oat kernels. Since it contains only a small amount of gluten, it is blended with other flours in recipes that require yeast. It combines well with wheat and rye flours and adds a chewy quality to desserts.

Rolled Oats—Shelled, sterilized, flattened oats. They are rich in minerals and protein. Used raw, rolled oats add a moist, sweet, and chewy texture to baked goods and are excellent in cookies and dessert bars. Used toasted, they add a crunchy texture and substitute well for nuts and seeds in recipes. Rolled oats may be whipped in a food processor or blender to produce oat flour.

Peanut Flour—Made from finely ground peanuts after most of the oil has been extracted. It substitutes well for a portion of the flour required in cakes, quick breads, and other baked products.

Rice Flour—Finely ground rice. It adds a grainy quality to baked goods and is most often substituted for wheat flour when an allergy to wheat is present. It may often be used as the only flour to produce crisp, light cookies.

Rye Flour—Finely ground rye. It is low in gluten, a rich dark color, and has a pleasantly distinctive flavor. Rye flour contributes fine texture and solidness to baked goods. It is often combined with other grains and is excellent as the predominant flour in crackers.

Soy Flour—A product of finely ground soybeans. It may be purchased raw, but it is often available toasted to a yellow color and distinctive nutty flavor. Soy flour is available with varying amounts of natural fat, but since the fat is rich in lecithin and vitamin E, it is nutritionally desirable. Also, lecithin and vitamin E act as natural preservatives in baked products, helping them retain freshness. Soy flour is also high in protein and B vitamins, and it lacks gluten. It is often added in small amounts to baked goods. Start with a tablespoon and increase the proportion to suit your taste.

Whole Wheat Flour—Made from the whole wheat berry. Stoneground whole wheat flour is preferred, since the flour is not exposed to the vitamin-destructive heat of steel grinding. It is a good source of B vitamins and protein, is rich in gluten, and has a pleasant flavor. Whole wheat flour is extremely versatile and is the primary flour in an increasing number of households.

Whole Wheat Pastry Flour—Ground soft grain wheat. (Whole wheat is usually hard wheat.) It is nutritionally comparable to whole wheat and in addition to substituting well for white flour in general baking, it is nutritionally far superior. Its very fine texture produces light pastries, cakes, and pie crusts, and it is recommended for desserts. It does tend to produce drier desserts when substituted completely for white flour, so begin with partial substitutions and judge each recipe separately.

APPENDIX III

CALORIC VALUES OF SUGAR, HONEY, AND FRESH FRUIT COMPARED*

One Cup	Aprox. Calories	% of Calories to Sugar	Compared to Honey
Sugar, granulated	751	100%	76%
Honey	992	132%	100%
Apple, diced	59	8%	6%
Apricot, halves	79	11%	8%
Banana, sliced	128	17%	13%
Blackberry, hulled	82	11%	8%
Blueberry, whole	90	12%	9%
Cantaloupe, cubed	48	6%	5%
Cherry, sweet	114	15%	11%
Cranberry, trimmed	52	7%	5%
Grape, whole	104	14%	10%
Grapefruit, pieces	78	10%	8%
Honeydew, diced	55	7%	6%
Mango, diced	108	14%	11%
Orange, pieces	118	16%	12%
Papaya, cubed	71	9%	7%
Peach, diced	102	14%	10%
Pear, sliced	100	13%	10%
Pineapple, diced	82	11%	8%

One Cup	Aprox. Calories	% of Calories to Sugar	Compared to Honey
Sugar, granulated	751	100%	76%
Honey	992	132%	100%
Plum, diced	78	10%	8%
Strawberry, whole	53	7%	5%
Tangerine, pieces	89	12%	9%
Watermelon, diced	42	6%	4%

*Average Caloric Value Per Cup of Fresh Fruit is only 82.

Caloric values per cup is from The U.S. Department of Agriculture.

APPENDIX IV

REFERENCE TABLE

EQUIVALENTS

Raisins—1 pound = 2⅜ cups whole
    4½ ounce package = 1 cup chopped
Nutmeats—1 pound = 2⅔ cups chopped
    5⅓ ounce can = 1 cup chopped
Dates—1 pound whole = 1¾ cups chopped
Figs—1 pound = 2⅔ cups chopped
Apples—1 pound = 3 cups sliced
Lemons—1 large = ¼ cup juice
    Rind of 1 whole = 1 tablespoon grated
Oranges—1 whole = 6 to 8 tablespoons juice
    Rind of 1 whole = 2 tablespoons grated

WEIGHTS AND MEASURES

3 teaspoons = 1 tablespoon	2 pints = 1 quart
4 tablespoons = ¼ cup	4 quarts (liquid) = 1 gallon
2 cups = 1 pint	1 lb. flour = 4 cups

SUBSTITUTIONS

If recipe calls for	*Substitute*
1 cup butter	⅞ cup oil
1 teaspoon baking powder	¼ teaspoon baking soda and ½ teaspoon cream of tartar
1 cup shortening	⅔ cup oil
1 cup buttermilk	Add 1½ T. lemon juice or vinegar to 1 cup milk
1 T. flour (for thickening)	½ T. cornstarch

145

APPENDIX V

NUTRITIONAL VALUES OF UNSWEETENED FRUIT JUICES

100 grams edible portion	Water (%)	Food Energy (calories)	Protein (grams)	Fat (grams)	Carbohydrates Total (grams)	Fiber (grams)	Calcium (mg.)	Phosphorus (mg.)	Iron (mg.)	Sodium (mg.)	Potassium (mg.)	Vitamin A (units)	Thiamine (mg.)	Riboflavin (mg.)	Niacin (mg.)	Vitamin C (mg.)
Apple juice (canned, bottled)	87.8	47	.1	T	11.9	.1	6	9	.6	1	101	—	.01	.02	.1	1
Apricot nectar (canned)	84.6	57	.3	.1	14.6	.2	9	12	.2	T	151	950	.01	.01	.2	3
Grapefruit (frozen, diluted)	89.3	41	.5	.1	9.8	T	10	17	.1	1	170	10	.04	.02	.2	39
Lemon (from frozen)	92.0	22	.4	.2	7.2	T	7	9	.3	1	141	20	.03	.01	.1	44

Lime (bottled)	90.3	26	.3	.1	9.0	T	9	11	.2	1	104	10	.02	.01	.1	21
Orange (frozen, diluted)	88.1	45	.7	.1	10.7	T	9	16	.1	1	186	200	.09	.01	.3	45
Peach nectar (canned)	87.2	48	.2	T	12.4	.1	4	11	.2	1	78	430	.01	.02	.4	T
Pear nectar (canned)	86.2	52	.3	.2	13.2	.3	3	5	.1	1	39	T	T	.02	T	T
Pineapple (frozen, diluted)	86.5	52	.4	T	12.8	.1	11	8	.3	1	136	10	.07	.02	.2	12

Note: T = Trace

Adapted from Agricultural Handbook No. 8, U.S. Dept. of Agriculture, 1963

NUTRITIONAL VALUES OF DRIED FRUITS

100 grams edible portion	Water (%)	Food Energy (calories)	Protein (grams)	Fat (grams)	Carbohydrates		Calcium (mg.)	Phosphorus (mg.)	Iron (mg.)	Sodium (mg.)	Potassium (mg.)	Vitamin A (units)	Thiamine (mg.)	Riboflavin (mg.)	Niacin (mg.)	Vitamin C (mg.)
					Total (grams)	Fiber (grams)										
Apples (dried)	24.0	275	1.0	1.6	71.8	3.1	31	52	1.6	5	569	—	.06	.12	.5	10
Apricots (dried)	25.0	260	5.0	.5	66.5	3.0	67	108	5.5	26	979	10,900	.01	.16	3.3	12
Banana (dehydrated)	3.0	340	4.4	.8	88.6	2.0	32	104	2.8	4	1477	760	.18	.24	2.8	7
Dates (dried)	22.5	274	2.2	.5	72.9	2.3	59	63	3.0	1	648	50	.09	.10	2.2	0
Figs (dried)	23.0	274	4.3	1.3	69.1	5.6	126	77	3.0	34	640	80	.10	.10	.7	0
Peaches (dried)	25.0	262	3.1	.7	68.3	3.1	48	117	6.0	16	950	3900	.01	.19	5.3	18
Pears (dried)	26.0	268	3.1	1.8	67.3	6.2	35	48	1.3	7	573	70	.01	.18	.6	7
Prunes (dried)	28.0	255	2.1	.6	67.4	1.6	51	79	3.9	8	694	1600	.09	.17	1.6	3

Adapted from Agricultural Handbook No. 8, U.S. Dept. of Agriculture, 1963

NUTRITIONAL VALUES OF FRESH FRUIT

100 grams edible portion	Water (%)	Food Energy (calories)	Protein (grams)	Fat (grams)	Carbohydrates		Calcium (mg.)	Phosphorus (mg.)	Iron (mg.)	Sodium (mg.)	Potassium (mg.)	Vitamin A (units)	Thiamine (mg.)	Riboflavin (mg.)	Niacin (mg.)	Vitamin C (mg.)
					Total (grams)	Fiber (grams)										
Apples (fresh, whole)	84.8	56	.2	.6	14.1	1.0	7	10	.3	1	110	90	.03	.02	.1	7
Apricots (raw)	85.3	51	1.0	.2	12.8	.6	17	23	.5	1	281	2700	.03	.04	.6	10
Avocado (raw)	74.0	167	2.1	16.4	6.3	1.6	10	42	.6	4	604	290	.11	.20	1.6	14
Banana (common)	75.7	85	1.1	.2	22.2	.5	8	26	.7	1	370	190	.05	.06	.7	10
Blueberry (raw)	83.2	62	.7	.5	15.3	1.5	15	13	1.0	1	81	100	.03	.06	.5	14
Cantaloupe (raw)	91.2	30	.7	.1	7.5	.3	14	16	.4	12	251	3400	.04	.03	.6	33

100 grams edible portion	Water (%)	Food Energy (calories)	Protein (grams)	Fat (grams)	Total (grams)	Fiber (grams)	Calcium (mg.)	Phosphorus (mg.)	Iron (mg.)	Sodium (mg.)	Potassium (mg.)	Vitamin A (units)	Thiamine (mg.)	Riboflavin (mg.)	Niacin (mg.)	Vitamin C (mg.)
Grape (raw)	81.6	69	1.3	1.0	15.7	.6	16	12	.4	3	158	100	.05	.03	.3	4
Grapefruit (raw)	88.4	41	.5	.1	10.6	.2	16	16	.4	1	135	80	.04	.02	.2	38
Guava (raw)	83.0	62	.8	.6	15	5.6	23	42	.9	4	289	280	.05	.05	1.2	242
Honeydew (raw)	90.6	33	.8	.3	7.7	.6	14	16	.4	12	251	40	.04	.03	.6	23
Lemon (raw)	87.4	20	1.2	.3	10.7	–	61	15	.7	3	145	30	.05	.04	.2	77
Lime (raw)	89.3	28	.7	.2	9.5	.5	33	18	.6	2	102	10	.03	.02	.2	37
Mango (raw)	81.7	66	.7	.4	16.8	.9	10	13	.4	7	189	4800	.05	.05	1.1	35
Orange (raw, peeled)	86.0	49	1.0	.2	12.2	.5	41	20	.4	1	200	200	.10	.04	.4	50

Papaya (raw)	88.7	39	.6	.1	10.0	.9	20	16	.3	3	234	1750	.04	.04	.3	56
Peach (raw)	89.1	38	.6	.1	9.7	.6	9	19	.5	1	202	1330	.02	.05	1.0	7
Pear (raw, skin)	83.2	61	.7	.4	15.3	1.4	8	11	.3	2	130	20	.02	.04	.1	4
Persimmon (raw)	64.4	127	.8	.4	33.5	1.5	27	26	2.5	1	310	–	–	–	–	66
Pineapple (raw)	85.3	52	.4	.2	13.7	.4	17	8	.5	1	146	70	.09	.03	.2	17
Plum (raw)	81.1	66	.5	T	17.8	.4	18	17	.5	2	299	300	.08	.03	.5	–
Pomegranate (raw)	82.3	63	.5	.3	16.4	.2	3	8	.3	3	259	T	.03	.03	.3	4
Strawberry (raw)	89.9	37	.7	.5	8.4	1.3	21	21	1.0	1	164	60	.03	.07	.6	59
Sweet Cherry (raw)	80.4	70	1.3	.3	17.4	.4	22	19	.4	2	191	110	.05	.06	.4	10

100 grams edible portion	Water (%)	Food Energy (calories)	Protein (grams)	Fat (grams)	Total (grams)	Fiber (grams)	Calcium (mg.)	Phosphorus (mg.)	Iron (mg.)	Sodium (mg.)	Potassium (mg.)	Vitamin A (units)	Thiamine (mg.)	Riboflavin (mg.)	Niacin (mg.)	Vitamin C (mg.)
Watermelon (raw)	92.6	26	.5	.2	6.4	.3	7	10	.5	1	100	590	.03	.03	.2	7

Note: T = Trace

Adapted from Agricultural Handbook No. 8, U.S. Dept. of Agriculture, 1963

APPENDIX VI

A FEW KITCHEN WEIGHTS, MEASURES, AND METRIC EQUIVALENTS

Metric conversions don't always work out in tidy round numbers because one must deal with decimals. For example, to convert ounces to grams, you multiply ounces by 28.35. However, should you wish to experiment with the metric system, the following simple tables give accepted equivalents for many of the quantities and ingredients used in this book.

		liquid	approximate grams
60 drops	1 teaspoon	⅙ oz.	
3 teaspoons	1 tablespoon	½ oz.	15 g.
4 tablespoons	¼ cup	2 oz.	60 g.
16 tablespoons	1 cup	8 oz.	225 g.
2 cups	1 pint	16 oz.	450 g. (1 lb.)
4 cups	1 quart	32 oz.	900 g. (2 lbs.)

Temperatures, Fahrenheit to Celsius

225 degrees F	110 degrees C
250 degrees F	120 degrees C
300 degrees F	150 degrees C
350 degrees F	180 degrees C
375 degrees F	190 degrees C

Inches to Centimeters

1 inch	2½ cm
1½ inches	4 cm
3 inches	8 cm
8 inches	20 cm

SUGGESTED READING

Abrahamson, E.M., and A.W. Pezet. *Body, Mind, and Sugar.* Moonachie, N.J.: Pyramid Publications/Harcourt Brace Jovanovich, 1971.

Benarde, Melvin A. *The Chemicals We Eat.* New York: American Heritage Press, 1971.

Davis, Adelle. *Let's Have Healthy Children.* New York: Harcourt Brace and World, 1954.

Dufty, William. *Sugar Blues.* New York: Warner Books, 1975.

Fredericks, Carlton, and Herman Goodman. *Low Blood Sugar and You.* New York: Constellation International, 1969.

Hunter, Beatrice Trum. *The Great Nutrition Robbery.* New York: Charles Scribner's Sons, 1978.

Smith, Lendon. *Feed Your Kids Right: Dr. Smith's Program for Your Child's Total Health.* New York: McGraw-Hill Book Co., 1979.

Turner, James S. *The Chemical Feast.* New York: Grossman Publishers, 1970.

U.S., Department of Agriculture. *Composition of Foods, Agricultural Handbook No. 8.* Washington, D.C.: Government Printing Office, 1963.

Yudkin, John. *Sweet and Dangerous: The New Facts about the Sugar You Eat as a Cause of Heart Disease, Diabetes, and Other Killers.* New York: Peter H. Wyden, 1972.

INDEX